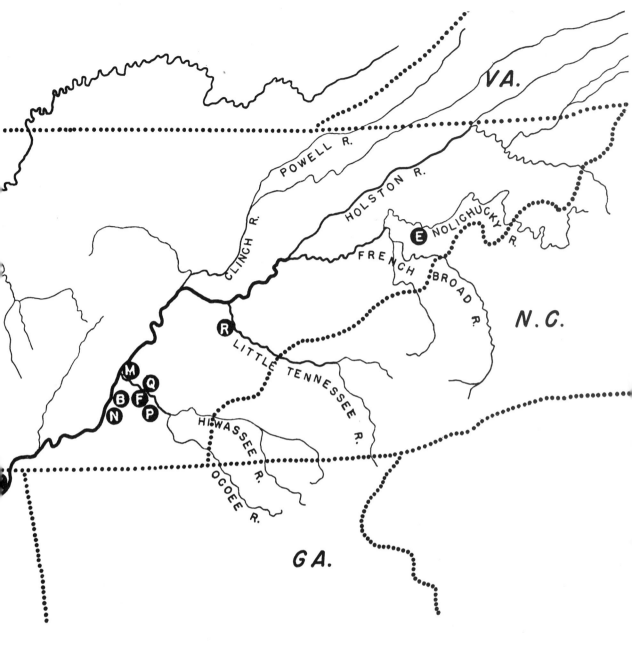

J   OBION RIVER TEMPLE MOUND SITE

K   SHILOH TEMPLE MOUND SITE

L   HARPETH RIVER TEMPLE MOUND SITE

M   HIWASSEE ISLAND SITE

N   TEMPLE MOUND SITE AT DALLAS ISLAND

O   FLINT QUARRIES

P   CHESTOWEE SITE

Q   LEDFORD ISLAND SITE

R   FORT LOUDOUN

S   DUCK RIVER SITE

Through the still lapse of ages. All that tread
The globe are but a handful to the tribes
That slumber in its bosom.

—WILLIAM CULLEN BRYANT

Tribes That Slumber

Indians of the
Tennessee Region

by

Thomas M. N. Lewis and Madeline Kneberg

illustrated by Madeline Kneberg

The University of Tennessee Press
Knoxville, Tennessee

Preface

This book has been written for students, for amateur archaeologists, and for all other persons with curiosity about the Indians.

The story is factual because it is based upon archaeological researches, both our own and those of our colleagues, and upon historical records. As we have gazed back into the faintly illuminated distant past, the people of our story have become almost like old friends to us. Our aim, insofar as it is possible, is to make them your friends too, and in so doing to breathe some life into the dust-covered facts of archaeology.

Within the decayed remains of ancient dwelling sites lie unwritten records of long forgotten peoples. The science of archaeology is dedicated to the recovery and interpretation of such records, to the end that the whole of human life may be better understood.

The entirety of mankind's past has been a drama of endless change, trial and error, historical accident and, in the very broadest sense, the survival of the fittest. For man has always found ways to cope with the forces of environment and to progress on the long road to civilization.

Written history covers only a brief span of the growth of human culture, while the unwritten records stretch far back into the remote past. Archaeology seeks to establish continuity between history and prehistory, and thereby contribute to an understanding of the essential nature of man and his behavior.

The data of archaeology are the products of past human behavior. The temples and dwellings that have all but turned to dust, the pottery vessels, the tools and the ornaments, and the crumbling bones of human skeletons are the material evidence. The activities of the people and the events which took place are reconstructed from these fragmentary remains of past cultures.

Contents

Illustrations

Acknowledgment is made by the authors and publisher to Herman K. Strauch for drawings of the following artifacts: four bone awls on page 28; weaving illustrations on page 88; pottery on pages 100 and 147; shell gorgets on page 111; one shell mask and the earpins on page 112; and the four pipes at the corners of the illustration on page 119.

Chapter 1

Nomadic Hunters
of the Ice Age

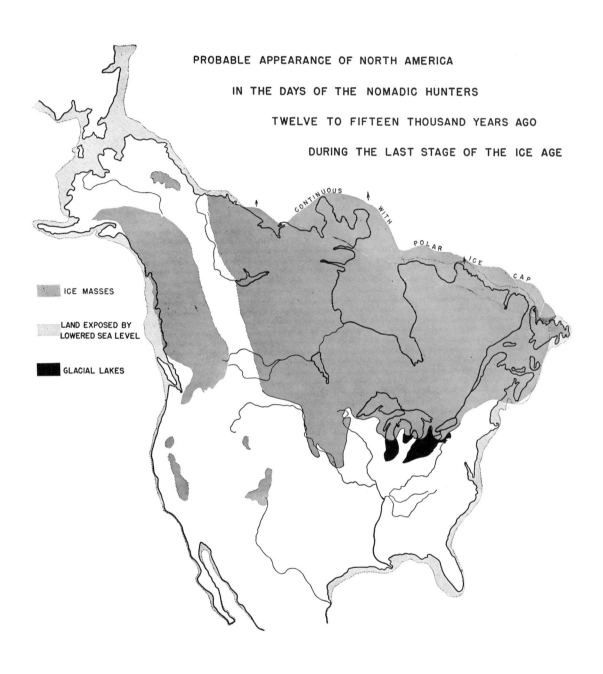

PROBABLE APPEARANCE OF NORTH AMERICA

IN THE DAYS OF THE NOMADIC HUNTERS

TWELVE TO FIFTEEN THOUSAND YEARS AGO

DURING THE LAST STAGE OF THE ICE AGE

CONTINUOUS WITH POLAR ICE CAP

ICE MASSES

LAND EXPOSED BY
LOWERED SEA LEVEL

GLACIAL LAKES

Nomadic Hunters of the Ice Age

When the last great Ice Age still held the world in its frozen grasp, human beings first gazed upon the green valley of the Tennessee River. It was at least fifteen thousand years ago or more that small bands of nomadic hunters ventured into the untrodden wilderness that never before had known the sound of a human voice. These people were akin to other Ice Age hunters who first populated the New World.

At that time North America was far different from today. Much of Canada and the present Great Lakes region of the United States were covered by a single ice mass, thousands of square miles in extent and hundreds of feet thick. Around the southern borders of this ice were immense glacial lakes, drained by the Mississippi River system. Another glacier covered the Canadian Rockies, and smaller ice masses capped the highest ranges of the American Rockies. Many of the present dry, or almost dry, basins of the western United States were lakes and marshes. In the eastern United States, near the glaciers, the vegetation varied from spruce-fir forests to birch woods and tundra. In the southeastern United States, forests of pine, hemlock, oak, chestnut and hickory flourished in a climate that was somewhat cooler and damper than the present.

The animal life of those times included many large species that are now extinct; among them were mammoths and mastodons, wild horses and camels, giant ground sloths and saber-toothed tigers, and large, straight-horned bison. Some of these animals lived on grassy plains, while others were native to the forests. The familiar modern species of wild game were much more abundant, because there were few people to hunt them and only their natural animal enemies to keep their numbers down.

Even the shapes of the continents were different at that time. This was because of the great glaciers throughout the northern latitudes in both the Old and New Worlds. To form the glaciers, moisture from the earth's atmosphere had accumulated as ice and snow. This process, which involved thousands of years, gradually lowered the level of the oceans as more and more of the moisture was held captive by the glaciers. At the maximum of the last glacial period, some twenty to thirty thousand years ago, sea level is estimated to have been as much as four hundred and fifty feet lower than at present. As recently as eleven thousand years ago it was a hundred feet lower. Depth soundings in Bering Sea show that when it was at the lowest stage, North America and Asia were connected by a broad rolling plain hundreds of miles wide from north to south.

Such was the nature of North America at the dawn of the New World's human history. As far as science can tell, there were no human beings in the Western Hemisphere before the last Ice Age glaciation, known as the Wisconsin. Throughout the world during the long Ice Age, all of mankind lived as nomadic hunters, camping in favorable spots where big game was plentiful and moving on when the migratory habits of the animals demanded it. For hundreds of thousands of years mankind had been developing a special human way of life. Thousands of generations had lived and died, learning to make more and more efficient tools and weapons, to sew animal skins into clothing, to live in social groups, and to speculate about the nature of life and death.

This human way of life is called "culture." Unlike the ways of life of other living things which are instinctive, the ways of human life must be learned. They must be taught to each and every person. Culture is the sum total of all of the ideas, beliefs, values and techniques that are passed from generation to generation. By the time of the last glacial period, culture had developed to the point that mankind could exist under all sorts of conditions, including the intense cold of the northern latitudes.

Thus it happened that Ice Age hunters, wandering in small groups composed of several related families, spread far and wide over the Old World. Eventually they reached the Arctic plain that connected Siberia with Alaska. From there they spread southward through Canada to the plains and virgin forests beyond. This did not happen in a generation, nor even in a century. Thousands of years passed before any considerable population accumulated in the New World.

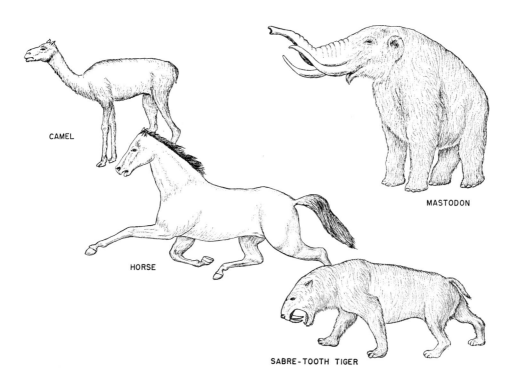

CAMEL

MASTODON

HORSE

SABRE-TOOTH TIGER

It was not until 1926 that archaeologists realized that man had migrated to the New World early enough to have hunted extinct animals. In that year, near Folsom, New Mexico, nineteen unusual flint spearpoints were found with the fossil bones of twenty-three bison. These bison, of a species that has been extinct for thousands of years, were straight-horned and larger than the modern species. The spearpoints, distinctive in having longitudinal grooves or flutings on both faces, are called Folsom points. The probable purpose of the fluting was to countersink the end of the spear shaft in order to streamline it for better penetration. By cutting a slot in the tapered end of a wooden shaft, the flint point could be inserted and secured with lashings. Besides providing for better penetration, this method of hafting helped to prevent breakage of the flint point, since it was reinforced for most of its length by the wood of the shaft. This provision was advantageous in hunting big game that had tough hides and thick fur.

In addition to the fluting feature, the Folsom and other early types of points often have the edges ground smooth where lashed to the shaft. Objects chipped from flint have sharp edges like broken glass, a property that makes them effective as weapons or

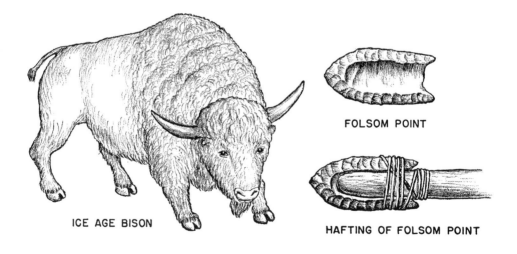

ICE AGE BISON

FOLSOM POINT

HAFTING OF FOLSOM POINT

cutting tools. But these same sharp edges had a tendency to cut lashings used to bind the point in place, hence grinding the edges smooth had a very practical purpose.

Since the days when the first fluted points were recognized as the handiwork of ancient hunters, thousands have been found throughout North America. Not all are exactly like the Folsom points which are rather small and delicate. At an ancient site near Clovis, New Mexico, larger fluted spearpoints have been found with bones of mammoths. These larger points, which are only partly fluted, are called Clovis points. The same type of spearpoints has been found with a mammoth's skeleton in southern Arizona. In both cases there was no doubt that the mammoths had been killed by the spearpoints. The Clovis point is the type that is usually found in the eastern United States, with most of the fluted points from the Tennessee region belonging to this type. They are most numerous in northern Alabama and the Highland Rim area of Tennessee. So far none has been found in the eastern United States with bones of either extinct or recent species of animals.

Not all of the spearpoints of the Ice Age hunters were fluted, nor were they the same shape as Clovis and Folsom points. In the Sandia Mountains of New Mexico, which form a part of the great mountain belt that stretches from Alaska to southern Mexico, one of the most ancient sites in the New World was discovered. This is a cave in which spearpoints, tools, and the fossilized bones of extinct animals were cemented into layers called breccia.

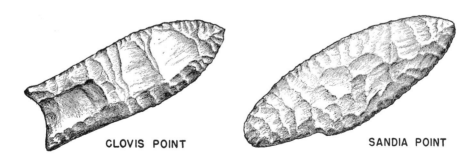

CLOVIS POINT   SANDIA POINT

These layers consisted of broken bits of limestone that had fallen from the ceiling of the cave and had become solidified into a mass by dripping water that carried limestone in solution. The lowest layer on the original floor of the cave contained the bones of horses, camels, mastodons, mammoths and bison. Lying among the bones were flint spearpoints, and near them were fireplaces still filled with charcoal where the meat had been cooked. The spearpoints have a slight stem formed by an indentation or notch on one side only. They are known as Sandia points.

The same cave was occupied at a later time by people who made Folsom fluted points. Quite some time elapsed between the abandonment of the cave by the original Sandia hunters and the occupation of the cave by the Folsom hunters. Both groups, and the Clovis people as well, were big game hunters and lived much the same sort of life.

Until recently, archaeologists had to rely upon their own calculated guesses or upon the estimates of geologists to tell them how long ago the ancient hunters roamed America. But, with the advent of the atomic age a new method of dating was devised, the result of the discovery that all living organisms, including both plants and animals, contain several kinds of carbon, one of which is radioactive. The radioactivity, which can be detected by a Geiger counter, begins to decay when the organism dies. Half of the radioactivity is lost after 5568 years, three-fourths after 11,136 years, and so on, the amount of radioactivity being determined by the number of counts per minute registered on a Geiger counter. By this method, charcoal from ancient camp fires and other organic materials found on archaeological sites can be dated.

A number of sites of the Ice Age hunters have been dated this way, the dates ranging from about ten thousand to more than twenty-five thousand years ago. Even the last advance of the glacial ice has been dated. In southern Wisconsin a spruce forest that was buried beneath the ice sheet and preserved in peat has been dated at about eleven thousand years ago.

Information about the Ice Age hunters is still meager, partly because they were nomadic and never lived long in any one spot, and partly because their worldly goods were few. Yet a number of their tools have been found, and from these can be drawn inferences concerning their way of life. Most of the tools were made from thin, flat blades of flint or similar stone. First, a flat surface was prepared on a nodule of stone. Then, a sharp and well-directed blow at the edge of this flat striking platform knocked off long, narrow blades that were thin and flat. Such blades were often used just as they were for knives, since the edges were as sharp as broken glass. When carefully examined, they show evidence of use which dulled the edge. Others were retouched (finely chipped) to produce a sharp edge. Most of the tools were retouched on one surface only, and for that reason are called "uniface" tools.

Scrapers were made from blades by chipping a steep cutting edge along the side or at the end. A common scraper type is trapezoidal in shape with the broadest edge forming the bit. Occasionally the corners of the bit end in sharp spurs. Since the scrapers were presumably used in preparing hides, these spurs may have served to slit the hides into usable sections. Such scrap-

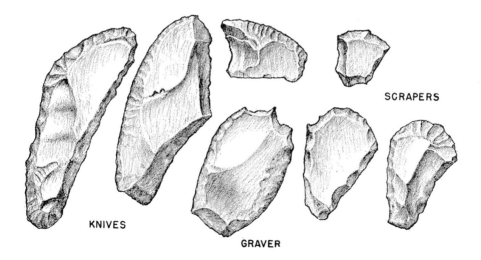

KNIVES

GRAVER

SCRAPERS

ers were probably also employed in working wood, bone and antler. The spurs in such instances may have been used for engraving decorations.

Some tools were merely small flakes with one or more finely chipped, delicate points. These are called gravers and may have been used for engraving. They may also have been utilized for punching small holes in skins that were to be laced together to make clothing and other equipment.

Flint drills for boring holes in wood, bone or antler have also been found, and occasionally rough chopping blades. In most of the ancient sites, nothing but stone tools and spearpoints has been preserved. However, in one Oregon cave, dated at more than nine thousand years ago, a fragment of woven basketry and many woven sandals have been found. Elsewhere a few bone tools have been recovered.

Ice Age hunters, whose technology included similar equipment, were the Tennessee region's first inhabitants. Hundreds of their fluted spearpoints and stone tools have been found throughout the region. Because they are particularly numerous in the Highland Rim area, it appears that this was one of their favorite hunting grounds. The Highland Rim is an upland that extends from northern Alabama across Middle Tennessee and up into Kentucky. Although the Tennessee, the Cumberland, and other smaller rivers flow through it, most of it is poorly watered, and the vegetation is less dense than in the lowlands. This condition, undoubtedly, was similar in Ice Age times. Since various species of prairie plants still grow there, the area may have been predominantly a grassland where herds of grazing animals congregated. Many isolated finds of fluted spearpoints have been found on the Rim, but no evidence of camping places. Yet in the adjacent lowlands along the rivers and streams, actual camp sites have been discovered.

One of the most important of these, in northern Alabama near Decatur, is known as the Quad site. Not only are fluted points very numerous on this site, but there is also a wide variety of scrapers, gravers, drills and choppers. Many other sites that were used as camping places by these people have been found in the same general area.

In eastern Tennessee a camp site of the Ice Age hunters has been found in Hamilton County and is known as the LeCroy site. Although only fifteen fluted points have been found there, the cutting and scraping tools number in the hundreds. Large camping places like the Quad and LeCroy sites may have been winter quarters to which the wandering bands returned year after year.

Elsewhere in Tennessee and adjacent northern Alabama, hundreds of fluted points have been found. So far, the following thirty-one Tennessee counties have yielded spearpoints made by their most ancient inhabitants: Bedford 15, Benton 8, Bledsoe 1, Blount 1, Cheatham 1, Coffee 1, Crockett 2, Davidson 4, Decatur 2, DeKalb 1, Dickson 1, Hamilton 28, Hardin 8, Henderson 2, Humphreys 3, Johnson 1, Knox 2, Madison 1, Maury 8, Meigs 2, Montgomery 1, Roane 1, Robertson 2, Rutherford 1, Smith 2, Sullivan 1, Sumner 20, Trousdale 2, Unicoi 1, Weakly 12, Williamson 6.

Many others, whose exact location by counties is unknown, have been found in the State. Seven of Alabama's northern counties—Franklin, Jackson, Lauderdale, Limestone, Madison, Marshall and Morgan—have produced at least a hundred fine examples of fluted points, and several thousand ancient tools of various types. Most of the spearpoints resemble the Clovis type used by the elephant hunters of the West. Remains of two elephant species, mammoth and mastodon, have been found in the Southeast at Natchez, Mississippi, and at Vero and Melbourne, Florida, under conditions that suggest hunters were present. Undoubtedly, the Tennessee region's first inhabitants also were hunters of elephants as well as other game.

So far no organic materials suitable for radiocarbon dating have been discovered on any of the Ice Age sites in the Tennessee region. However, in Russell Cave in northern Alabama the re-

FLUTED SPEARPOINTS FROM THE TENNESSEE REGION

mains of a later group have been dated at more than eight thousand years ago. Evidence of these later people overlies that of the Ice Age hunters at the Quad site in Alabama. There is good reason, therefore, to believe that man reached the Tennessee region long before the end of the Ice Age which lasted until about nine thousand years ago.

These early hunting bands were not large, yet the bands themselves must have been numerous to have penetrated into almost every nook and cranny of the New World. They may have been partly responsible for the extinction of some of the game animals, not only because they hunted them with weapons, but also because they deliberately set fires to stampede the animals into swamps, over cliffs, or into narrow gorges. Destruction of vegetation by extensive grass fires or forest fires would have upset the sensitive relationship which exists between animals and their food supply.

Perhaps the final factor which led to the extinction of the mammoths, mastodons, horses, camels and straight-horned bison was a drastic change in climate. Geologists and other scientists who have studied the changes in climate since the last Ice Age suggest that by nine thousand years ago when the glaciers began to shrink rapidly, the climate of North America was still somewhat colder and more moist than it is today. By seven thousand years ago it had become much warmer and drier than at present, and this condition lasted until about four thousand years ago. This warm, dry period is known as the Altithermal. It was a time when rainfall decreased and caused the lakes, streams and marshes to become smaller, or to disappear completely in many areas. The great, grassy plains of the West were the first to show pronounced effects. The eastern United States was also affected, with previously wooded uplands gradually turning into prairies, and many of the broad rivers becoming narrower and shallower.

Warm, dry periods were as important as Ice Age periods in influencing plants, animals and human beings. Even a relatively small cycle of drought years will drastically affect vegetation,

destroying forests and grasslands alike, and resulting in erosion
and dust storms. During the great drought of the Altithermal
period every permanent spring and watercourse was a concentration point for men and animals. The extinction of many of America's ancient big game species may have been the result of a combination of the drought which reduced their feeding grounds,
and the hunters who preyed upon them at the diminishing water-
ing places.

Although the large Ice Age animals became extinct, there is
no reason to suppose that the early hunters did not survive. For
man has always been able to adapt himself through his culture
to drastic changes in environment. Other species of game were
still plentiful in many parts of the New World, and the hunting
bands gradually dispersed in search of them. Many descendants
of the Ice Age hunters survived as small bands that participated
very little in the subsequent history of the New World. They
lived isolated in the more remote areas while other tribes from
Asia with new and different cultures were populating the Western Hemisphere. Many other bands became absorbed into the
new groups and thus lost their cultural identity. To the racial
composition of the American Indian, the Ice Age hunters con-
tributed their share. They are often called the Paleo-Indians, a
name which implies that they were the most ancient of the American Indians. Theirs was a Paleolithic (Old Stone Age) culture.

Very little is known about the physical appearance of these
people because remains of their skeletons are very scarce. Furthermore, the experts have not been willing to accept all of the
finds as authentic bones of Paleo-Indians. An exception to this is
a partial skeleton discovered near Midland, Texas, in 1953. De-
tailed, scientific studies of this find have shown that the skeleton
belongs to a period earlier than that of the Folsom culture which
has been dated as about ten thousand years old. The bones represent a young woman about thirty years of age at the time of her
death. Neither this skull nor those of any other supposed early
finds show significant differences from later American Indians.

They vary from each other just as the later Indians do. At least eight different physical varieties among the recent American Indians have been recognized. Some of these may represent different migrations of people from various Asiatic regions; others may have originated from mixtures between varieties, and still others may have developed in the New World as the result of isolation and inbreeding. These varieties do not correspond to tribes, although in some tribes a certain variety may predominate. Time will undoubtedly bring to light more skeletons of the Ice Age hunters, and the future may reveal just how they fit into the racial picture of the American Indian.

When the Ice Age ended and another chapter began in the prehistory of the New World, these ancient hunters no longer continued to dominate the scene. History moved on, and another people supplanted them.

Chapter 2

The Archaic Era

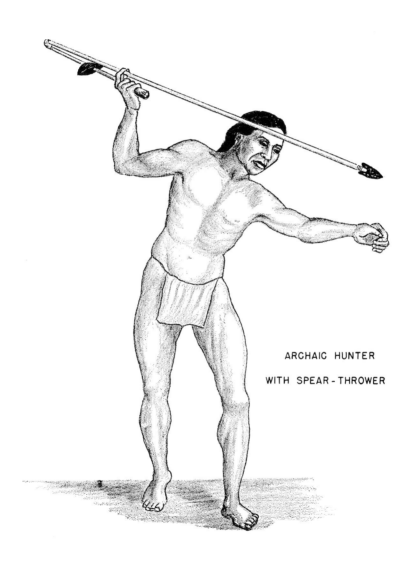

ARCHAIC HUNTER

WITH SPEAR-THROWER

FACIAL FEATURES RECONSTRUCTED OVER THE SKULL OF AN
ARCHAIC MAN WHO LIVED FIVE THOUSAND YEARS AGO

The Archaic Era

Out of the northern forests of Asia came another immigration to the New World. They were people whose way of life had become modified in response to changes in environment and through the accumulation of human knowledge. As the Ice Age waned, the forest belt had moved northward. These forests offered new resources to mankind. Plant foods such as nuts, fruits and seeds were abundant, and large and small game thrived. The rivers teemed with fish and contained inexhaustible quantities of shellfish. Such an environment offered rewards for a settled existence, rewards that were greater and more secure than those from nomadic hunting in earlier times.

Settled existence made it possible to have more permanent and more substantial dwellings. Some degree of leisure time for the development of technology became available. New techniques and new inventions not only increased man's ability to cope with his environment, but also made possible a greater development in the arts, philosophy and religion. Settled existence was an important step on the road leading to civilization.

The nomadic hunters of the Ice Age belonged to the Old Stone Age, while the settled hunters of the post-glacial forests belonged to an intermediate Stone Age called the Mesolithic. The security of this new way of life greatly increased the number of human beings in the world. In consequence, the Mesolithic hunters and fishermen spread far and wide along the streams and sea coasts of the Old World. Although the land connection that had existed in Ice Age times between Asia and Alaska disappeared with the melting of glaciers and the rising sea level, the shore of the New World was still visible from Asia. In between were the Diomede Islands to serve as steppingstones by which these people migrated to a new continent.

As time passed, these new people spread throughout the Americas, settling along coasts, on the shores of glacial lakes and along the banks of the great inland rivers. These people have come to be known as the Archaic Indians. They were made up of many tribes who spoke different tongues, but they shared a basic way of life—the Archaic culture. In some regions they lived in caves, and elsewhere in crudely constructed huts.

The Archaic era was a long one, lasting for thousands of years. It began some nine thousand years ago before the Paleo-Indian era ended, and lasted in isolated places up to the coming of the white man. In the Tennessee region, where it began at least eight thousand years ago, it lasted six thousand years or more.

Throughout these millennia the Archaic culture did not remain the same. It changed from within as local groups developed skills and new ideas of their own. It changed also from without, for eventually new and later cultures appeared from which ideas diffused. All cultures grew by borrowing much from others. And so the pattern of any individual culture, traced through time, is an ever-changing design. Within the design, one may recognize many basic elements that persist. Yet, intricately interwoven with them, appear new elements that cannot always be traced to their sources.

Such was the pattern of culture of the Archaic era in the Tennessee region. Its fundamental nature—the way in which the people achieved survival in their environment—remained unchanged. Nevertheless, in western Tennessee alone, six minor sub-patterns of the Archaic culture can be discerned. These differ from each other in some cases because they existed at different times. In other cases, the differences may be explained by local developments and influences from neighboring peoples.

The basic Archaic way of life in Tennessee, which is dated by radiocarbon as 7150 ± 500 years ago (about 5200 B.C.), is characterized by that of the "Eva" group. The designation "Eva" comes from one of their main settlements near the junction of Cypress Creek and the Tennessee River in Benton County, near the present hamlet of Eva. In those days, the channel of the river was not the same as in recent years. The settlement was a mile west of the recent channel prior to the building of Kentucky Dam, and was situated on an old, natural levee which formed the river bank at the time. Fresh water clams were abundant in the river and plenty of game was available in the forest. Also in the forest were nuts, fruits and roots to round out a balanced diet.

The Eva settlements were small; each included a habitation area and a single large trash heap which also served as a cemetery. The trash heaps were mainly composed of discarded clam shells, whenever the settlements were located near clam beds. Other garbage and the general refuse were also assigned to the same heaps which, through the centuries, grew into large mounds that covered hundreds of square feet. Much of the knowledge about the Archaic Indians has been gained from the graves contained in the trash heaps.

Dwellings of a rather substantial type were built, but nothing is known about structural details. The substantial nature of the dwellings was revealed during archaeological excavation when the discovery was made of molds of sturdy upright posts used as walls and roof supports. A postmold is a cylindrically shaped impression in the soil left by a decayed wooden post. It is nearly always darker in color and looser than the surrounding soil. The sizes of postmolds, their shapes and arrangements in patterns are a particularly valuable kind of archaeological evidence that has furnished a great deal of knowledge about prehistoric dwellings.

The postmolds of Archaic houses were about six inches in diameter, but so many houses had been built, generation after generation, that the original patterns of arrangement were obscured by the very great number of the postmolds.

Cooking was done outside the dwellings over open fires and in roasting pits. Many plant foods were probably dried in the sun to preserve them for winter use, but others such as acorns were slowly roasted in pits with heated rocks. Clams were baked in fireplaces on the refuse heaps, the fireplaces being merely bowl-shaped depressions scooped out for temporary use. No traces of any containers that might have been used for cooking have remained. However, containers of rawhide, wood, or tightly woven baskets are known to have been used for cooking by peoples with simple cultures, the water in such containers being heated to the boiling point by dropping in hot rocks.

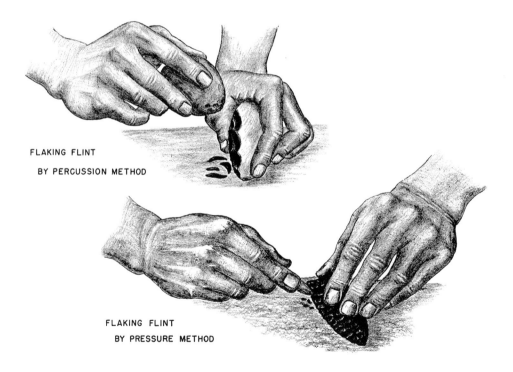

FLAKING FLINT
BY PERCUSSION METHOD

FLAKING FLINT
BY PRESSURE METHOD

All of the various cutting tools and most of the weapon points used by Archaic Indians were chipped from flint or similar stone. They worked the stone in two different ways. The main method was the Old World Paleolithic technique of percussion and pressure flaking. In percussion flaking the flint is battered into shape with skillful blows from a hammerstone; in pressure flaking a pointed tool of antler or bone is pressed against the edge to remove small flakes. Greater precision in shaping and sharpening tools is afforded by the pressure flaking technique. Both flaking techniques were adapted to working flint or similar stone that fractured readily.

The other main method of working stone is by pecking and grinding. This was usually employed for types of stone that did not fracture easily. While ground stone tools were not common until the Neolithic (New Stone Age), the technique of grinding stone was discovered in late Paleolithic times in the Old World where it was used in making statuettes and a few other items. The technique probably grew out of the earlier methods of grinding

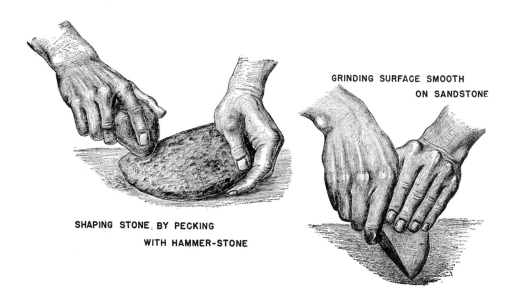

SHAPING STONE, BY PECKING
WITH HAMMER-STONE

GRINDING SURFACE SMOOTH
ON SANDSTONE

and polishing ivory and antler, but its application to hard, fine-grained stone was a distinct advance in man's ever progressing standards of workmanship. The Archaic Indians employed primarily the flaking method, but the grinding method was also a part of their technology, although applied to only a few items.

Flint tools were principally used in working wood, antler, bone and hides. The tools themselves have survived; so have the objects made of bone and antler, but wood and leather objects have long since turned to dust. Yet, evidence of these things can sometimes be inferred. For example, the high polish on the cutting edges of flint adzes indicates long-continued use in cutting and scraping wood. Hollowed-out log canoes were probably made just as they were by historic Indians, by alternately burning and

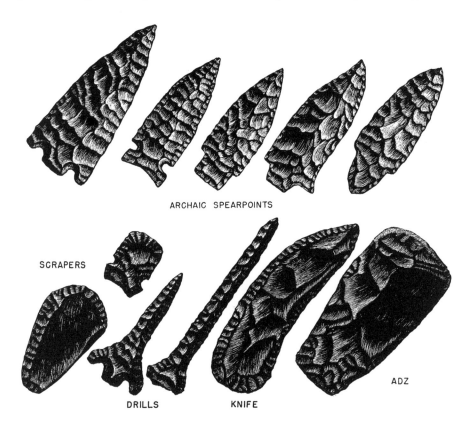

ARCHAIC SPEARPOINTS

SCRAPERS

DRILLS   KNIFE

ADZ

scraping away the charred wood. Large numbers of flint drills were used for boring holes in wood and other materials, and flint scrapers added the finishing touches to wooden, bone and antler objects. Flint scrapers also removed the flesh and hair from hides.

Most numerous of all the flint artifacts were the weapon points. Most of them were large, even larger than those used by the Paleo-Indians for killing mammoths, yet the largest game animals hunted by the Archaic Indians were elk and bears. The Archaic Indians used a variety of notches and stems for securing the points to the shafts of the spears. Starting with a basic triangular or oval blade, often well finished by pressure flaking, they made notches at the base, or on the sides near the base, or by removing both basal corners. Thus a variety of shapes was created.

A device called a spear-thrower was a characteristic Archaic weapon that had been invented in the Old World perhaps thirty thousand years ago. The earliest known examples come from the European area and are made of antler or ivory, elaborately carved. This device extended the length of the throwing arm, thus increasing the force and distance to which a spear could be cast. While no evidence of its use by Paleo-Indians has been discovered, it is probable that it was an indispensable part of their hunting equipment too. If it had been entirely made of wood, it could hardly have survived until today. There is no doubt about the use of the spear-thrower by the Archaic people. Certain parts of the device, made from antler and stone, have been found in graves, lying in positions that indicate the nature of the weapons. In a typical instance, a socketted section of antler with a small spur or hook was found lying about eighteen inches away from a perforated, polished stone object. Apparently these two objects had been connected by a wooden rod which, judging from the size of the socket and the perforation, was a little over a half inch in diameter. Assuming that a portion of the rod was used for a handle, the spear-thrower was at least two feet long.

The purpose of the polished stone objects on the spear-throwers is somewhat of a mystery. From a practical standpoint they may have been counterbalancing weights, moved to different positions along the rod, according to the weight of the spear to be thrown. On the other hand, and perhaps just as practical so far as the hunter was concerned, they may have been good luck charms. They were often made from attractively colored or unusual stone in a variety of shapes. It is certain that many hours of patient labor went into their production. They were not only symmetrically shaped and highly polished, but were drilled by a tedious method—a primitive version of core drilling, using a section of hollow reed and wet sand. The rapid rotation of the reed between the palms of the hands and the cutting action of the sand eventually perforated the hardest types of stone. This critical drilling operation demanded great skill because it was usually done after the object had been shaped. Incompletely drilled examples have revealed this sequence of manufacture.

Good weapons were indispensable for people whose subsistence and technology were largely dependent upon the hunting of animals. Yet they did not live by meat alone. Plants provided as important a part of their diet as plant life does for man today. Seeds and nuts, fruits and roots were gathered in quantity during the seasons of their ripening. Although baskets and other equip-

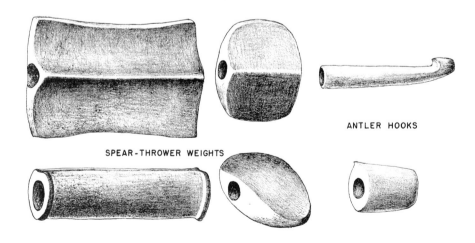

ANTLER HOOKS

SPEAR-THROWER WEIGHTS

ment used for gathering and storage have disappeared, stone pestles for pounding and grinding up seeds, nuts and roots have endured. The pestles were made of hard stone, but they gradually wore down with use, adding grit to the food in the process. During a lifetime of eating such gritty food, an Indian's teeth were worn down to the gums.

Fishing offered another means of securing food. Perhaps a great many fish were caught with spears, traps or nets, but the hook and line method was also used. Fishhooks were made of bone in an ingenious and practical way. Deer toe bones were sawed in half lengthwise, then the central portion of each half was removed and the remainder easily shaped into a strong hook.

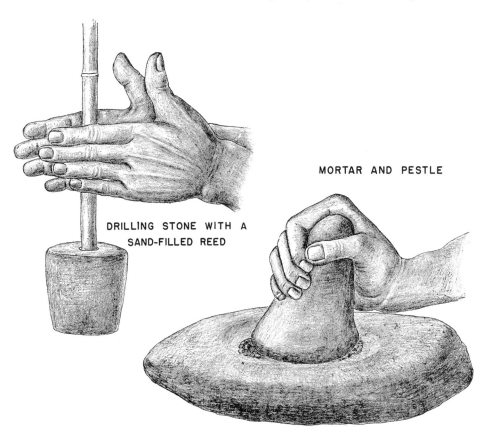

MORTAR AND PESTLE

DRILLING STONE WITH A
SAND-FILLED REED

The bones, antlers and teeth of animals were the raw materials for tools and ornaments. Many of the bone tools were employed in leather working. The processing of hides and the fashioning of them into clothing, footwear, bedding, containers, straps and thongs formed a major industry, probably engaged in by women exclusively and almost continuously. It is a craft, already ancient in the days of the Archaic Indians, whose modern practice grew out of painstaking, trial-and-error experiments of forgotten peoples. The common Indian method of preparing hides was to stretch the skin on the ground and scrape it clean, removing the flesh with bone or antler scrapers, and the hair with flint blades. The usual tanning was merely a matter of smearing the hide with the fat, brains and liver of the animal and then soaking it in water overnight. Sometimes, the skin was also smoked. Next, it was stretched on a pole framework to dry, and finally made

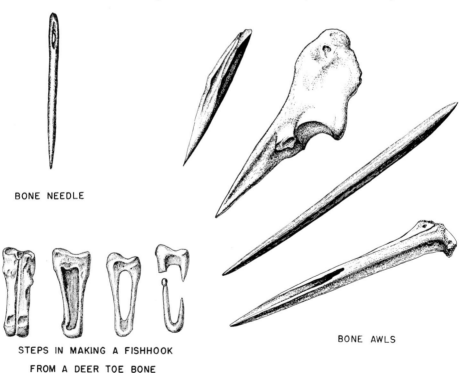

BONE NEEDLE

STEPS IN MAKING A FISHHOOK
FROM A DEER TOE BONE

BONE AWLS

pliable by working between the hands or sliding back and forth across a pole.

While flint knives were the cutting tools used in leather work, all of the assembling was done with bone awls and needles. The basic form of the needle, even to the elongated eye, invented in Paleolithic times in the Old World, has not changed today, except with respect to the material from which it is made. The large number of bone awls found on Archaic Indian sites indicates that leather was very important in the daily life of the people. Bone tools were also used for weaving various kinds of plant fibers into baskets, mats, bags and robes. Dry caves in the Ozark Mountains that were inhabited by Archaic Indians have contained many examples of preserved woven fabrics.

While bone was mostly used to make perforating tools, the antlers of deer and elk provided a tough material for stouter

SNAKE'S BACKBONE AND BOBCAT TEETH MADE INTO NECKLACES

tools and equipment. Among these were heavy tools for defleshing hides, handles for flint tools, and flakers for flint working. Occasionally, weapon points were made from sharpened and socketted antler tips.

Concerning the nature of clothing and ornaments there is little information. The finest handicrafts—the most colorful part of Archaic culture—were made of perishable materials. The clothes, paints and feathers have left no traces of their existence, except for a few small heaps of red ocher paint found in graves. Some of the ornaments made of stone, bone, shell and copper hint of the Archaic Indians' ideas of adornment. Bone bracelets were made from animal rib bones; the backbones of snakes were sometimes strung on cords to serve as ready-made necklaces. Among other odd items strung for necklaces were bear and bobcat eye teeth and turtle thigh bones. Some of the bone ornaments were decorated with engraving. Marine shell and copper ornaments have occasionally been found but were rare because the shells had to come from the distant Gulf of Mexico and the copper

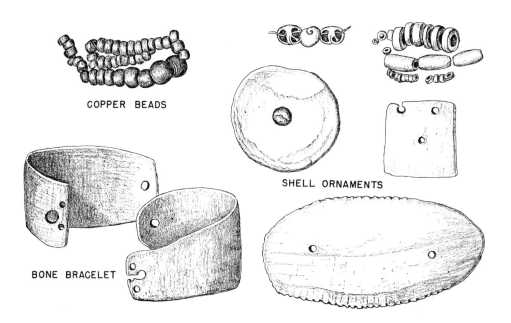

COPPER BEADS

SHELL ORNAMENTS

BONE BRACELET

from the Lake Superior region. Small shells were merely perforated, while large conchs were cut up and made into beads of various sizes.

The use of copper does not mean that these people knew the processes of metallurgy; they merely pounded copper nuggets into flat sheets that could be cut with flint knives. Some pieces were tightly rolled and then pounded and bent into the desired shapes. Very rarely, copper was made into fishhooks and awls; more often it was used for beads or other ornaments. The use of the metal at all by these ancient Tennesseans implies a familiarity with faraway regions and their resources. Marine shells and copper, however, were not used by the early Eva group. More than a thousand years passed before their descendants became

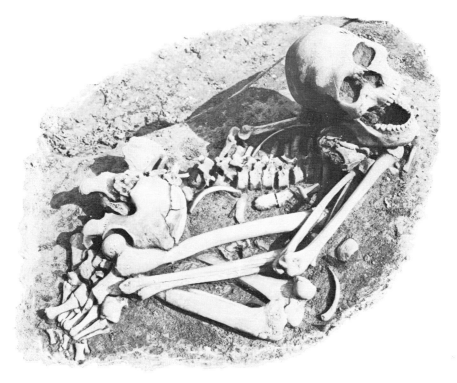

TYPICAL ARCHAIC BURIAL OF A MAN

acquainted with and sought out such materials.

While the long-inhabited Archaic villages indicated that life was relatively secure, it was, nonetheless, an existence that required ceaseless activity on the part of every able-bodied person. Each family was to a large extent self-sufficient, providing its own food, shelter, clothing, tools and weapons. A settlement was made up of a small group of such families, banded together for mutual aid and protection, and possessing a common burial ground.

Although the burial ground was usually the refuse heap, the careful treatment of the dead implies emotions of strong affections, as well as a belief in an afterlife. The arms and legs of a corpse were tightly folded against the body and bound in place. Ornaments and other intimate possessions were placed with the body to accompany the owner to the next world. The graves, small circular pits dug into the shell mounds, were seldom disturbed by any later digging, suggesting that they may have been marked in some manner. Sometimes a pet dog was buried in the grave with its former owner—perhaps intentionally killed so that its spirit could accompany that of its master in the afterlife.

Dogs were the first animals to be domesticated by man, probably during the latter part of the Paleolithic, and were immigrants from the Old World just as the Archaic Indians, their masters, were. The high regard in which dogs were held by these people may be inferred from the careful burial that they received, either with their owners or in separate graves. This regard may have arisen from services rendered by the dogs in hunting and as beasts of burden, or it may simply reveal the human response to the dogs' faithful and affectionate companionship.

Few Archaic individuals lived to be middle-aged according to our standards. Many died in their twenties and thirties—those who survived until fifty were the exception. From the evidence of their skeletons, their two greatest miseries were abscessed teeth and arthritis. While tooth decay was rare, root abscesses were common, due to excessive wear from gritty food exposing the tooth pulp, and from pyorrhea which loosened the teeth. The arthritis that attacked all of their joints and especially their spines has plagued the human species for ten thousand generations or more.

In appearance, some of the Archaic Indians most closely resembled the historic Sioux of the western plains. But there were at least two distinct types. One was broad-headed, broad-faced, square-jawed, and had a rather narrow, high-bridged nose; the other had a narrower and longer head, a narrower face, and was generally less rugged in bony structure. The women were small and usually showed more prognathism (forward projection of the mouth region) than the men.

These were the Archaic Indians and this was their way of life as lived in Eva times, and generally throughout the six thousand

BURIAL OF A DOG

years of their era (5200 B.C. to after the birth of Christ). During
that long time their culture changed. The Eva phase of culture
changed slowly into the "Three Mile" phase which differs only
through the acquiring of a few new things such as copper, and
through changes in styles of traditional weapon points and tools.
The people of the Three Mile phase were descendants of the
Eva people and lived in the same locality.

Prehistoric peoples and their cultures must be arbitrarily
named by archaeologists, because such peoples are always anon-
ymous. Neither the names they used for themselves nor those
used by their neighbors and contemporaries have endured. In
selecting a name, archaeologists usually choose that of some
modern landmark. Hence "Three Mile" comes from Three Mile
Slough, the modern name for an old river bed near the Eva site.

The Three Mile phase lasted from about 4000 B.C. until 1200
B.C. This was during the warm period known as the Altithermal.
At the end of this period, the world's climate became cooler and
damper, ushering in the period known as the Medithermal.
Heavier rainfall flooded out many of the shoals where the people
had collected clams. Although this deprived them of one of their
most important foods, the Archaic Indians continued to live in
the region. This change in climate also tended to cause some
groups in the northern United States to shift their habitat southward. Some of these were not Archaic Indians, but rather peoples
of a still more advanced stage of culture. From them the Archaic Indians borrowed ideas that are reflected in the next
period by new elements appearing in their culture. Thus, the
Three Mile was supplanted by the Big Sandy phase.

The Big Sandy, the final phase of the basic pattern that began
in Eva times, was named for the Big Sandy River which flows
into the Tennessee in Henry County. This phase reveals many
new items. Grooved axes, made by the grinding process, represent a new type of tool. Polished stone ornaments called gorgets
were used for adornment. Tubular stone pipes, perhaps used by
medicine men, appeared. Some, if not all, of these represent

borrowed ideas. Also, and of great importance, was the appearance of pottery obtained in trade from the new peoples. In some places the Archaic Indians actually learned to make pottery.

The Eva, Three Mile, and Big Sandy phases appear to be a single development of a pattern of life through time. The people might be thought of as a tribe whose descendants carried on the traditional pattern with slight changes from generation to generation and from century to century.

Other Archaic "tribes" such as this existed in the Tennessee Valley and the Southeast. Even within western Tennessee occurred another sequence of phases, the Kays, Weldon, and Ledbetter. The earliest was the Kays phase that dates back to about 3000 B.C. Although it existed at the time of the Three Mile phase, it differed in details of tool and weapon point styles and in certain customs. Dogs, for example, were not buried in separate graves nor with their masters. This custom, however, was bor-

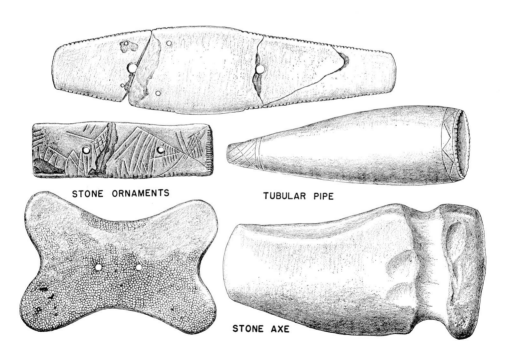

STONE ORNAMENTS   TUBULAR PIPE

STONE AXE

rowed later by descendants of the Kays people.

The Weldon phase represents an intermediate period that began about 2000 B.C. During it, some new variations in culture appeared. It lasted until about 1200 B.C. when the next phase, the Ledbetter, developed. This new phase corresponded in time to the Big Sandy. They shared many things in common, but still remained distinct from each other, as if they were the culture of different but neighboring tribes.

The Archaic era which began at the end of the Ice Age, during what is known as the Anathermal period when the world's climate was gradually warming, endured through the Altithermal and Medithermal periods in the Tennessee region. But finally, the Archaic way of life, a Mesolithic type of culture, was supplanted by Neolithic (New Stone Age) cultures. Like their predecessors, the Paleo-Indians, some of the Archaic peoples dispersed to isolated areas elsewhere while others were absorbed by groups of newcomers. As they faded from the scene of Tennessee's past, their place was taken by the bearers of Neolithic culture.

Chapter 3

Early Woodland Indians

FACIAL FEATURES RECONSTRUCTED OVER THE
SKULL OF A WOODLAND MAN WHO LIVED
ABOUT TWO THOUSAND YEARS AGO

Early Woodland Indians

Once more, Asia, the great reservoir of human population, released its overflow to the New World. Neolithic peoples, traveling the age-old route across Bering Strait to North America, found new homes. The simplest and earliest of the Neolithic cultures in North America is called the "Woodland" pattern, the name indicating the main area in which the culture occurs, the eastern woodlands. This vast area, from Canada to the Gulf, includes the eastern half of America in which coniferous forests blend imperceptibly into hardwoods.

Neolithic culture developed eight to ten thousand years ago in the Old World, probably in the Near East between Palestine and Turkestan. Basically, it was a revolutionary change in man's relationship to nature, because the true Neolithic introduced the domestication of plants and animals, thus emancipating mankind from the uncertainties of wild food supplies. Many arts and crafts that appeared at the same time were the consequence of the leisure and security afforded by the new way of life. Neolithic populations increased rapidly, often at the expense of their more primitive neighbors. Yet Neolithic inventions spread faster than the populations, and some ideas were borrowed by peoples who still lived by hunting and collecting. Among such inventions were: the technique of grinding stone, the true loom for weaving, and the making of pottery. The bow and arrow, which may have been invented much earlier, was greatly improved during the Neolithic. Its use spread over much of the world, supplanting among most peoples the more ancient spear-thrower.

The early Woodland Indians possessed many of the Neolithic inventions, but they had no domesticated animals except dogs, and evidence is sparse for domesticated plants. However, maize or Indian corn had been domesticated in Middle America very early and had spread to the southwestern United States by 1500 B.C. Corn, second only to wheat as a matrix out of which civilizations were born, is a domesticated grass like wheat. Unlike wheat, whose various wild forms still grow in many places, corn has no known wild ancestor. Its origin is shrouded in mystery, notwithstanding that the Indians grew hundreds of varieties. The most ancient examples that have been found belonged to the popcorn type with small, flinty kernels. Each separate kernel on the small cobs was covered with a husk. Botanists believe that a still earlier ancestor may have borne its kernels in the tassels instead of on cobs.

During centuries of Indian cultivation, the primitive type of maize changed until an amazing array of varieties existed at the time Columbus discovered America. Special kinds were used for meal, for flour, for popping and for corn-on-the-cob. The kernels came in assorted colors: black, yellow, red, white and blue. Moreover, there were varieties adapted to deserts, jungles and lofty mountains. Within two generations after Columbus, the new grain was grown in Europe and had spread to China. In modern civilization it not only provides food for man and beast, but it is also the raw material for an untold number of manufactured products. What wonder, then, that most Indians regarded corn with reverence and offered the first fruits of each harvest to their supreme gods.

Charred cobs and kernels that have been found in ancient sites of Woodland Indians in Ohio and Illinois prove that corn was grown in quantity two thousand years ago. So it is logical to suppose that the first cultivation of corn in the eastern United States was much earlier, and that most of the Woodland Indians were growing it by the beginning of the Christian era.

The Woodland Indians in the Tennessee region lived in small villages much like those of the Archaic peoples. Their dwellings were circular huts built of small saplings stuck in the ground and bent together to form a dome-shaped framework. The outside was covered with bark or mats, except perhaps for a small hole in the center of the roof that allowed smoke to escape. Some of the houses were as small as ten feet in diameter, while others were somewhat larger.

Similar dwellings, called "wigwams" by the Algonkin Indians, were still in use among descendants of Woodland tribes when the white man came. Early historic accounts describe the wigwams as the sleeping quarters for large families that included as many as twenty persons. Sleeping on mats and skins with their feet near the banked embers of the fire, men, women and children crowded into a single smoky wigwam where no one could move without disturbing others.

Except in the coldest days of winter, the Woodland Indians spent most of the day outside their wigwams. Cooking was mostly over open fires, but each family also had an underground oven. This was a kettle-shaped pit in the ground, smaller at the top than at the bottom, and large enough to roast a bushel or two of food at a time. Heat was supplied by a layer of glowing charcoal and pre-heated stones in the bottom of the pit. The lid for this oven was a large slab of bark which was sealed over with earth. Such underground ovens were used principally for roasting foods in order to preserve them, rather than for ordinary cooking.

Pottery vessels, used for most of the cooking, were enormous kettles that held up to five gallons. These vessels were made from local clays to which sand or ground-up rock had been added to prevent shrinkage and cracking during the process of manufacture. This process started with a mass of wet clay mixed with the rock. First, a long roll was made and coiled spirally to form a

conical bottom for the vessel. Then, additional rolls were added
as rings, one at a time, until the vessel was the desired height
and size. During this step, each coil of clay was firmly welded
to the previous one before another was added. Next, the inside
surface was scraped smooth and the walls thinned down until
they were one-fourth to one-half inch in thickness. During the
following step, the vessel, still moist and flexible, was beaten on
the outer surface with a paddle wound with cords or wrapped in
woven fabric. The paddling produced a roughened surface which
retained the impressions of the cords or fabric. This surface
finish was not particularly ornamental, but its roughness was
practical because the vessel, after long use in cooking, became
greasy and slippery. After the surface was finished, the damp
vessel was dried in the sun. Then came the critical firing operation which involved gradual pre-heating near a hot fire, and final

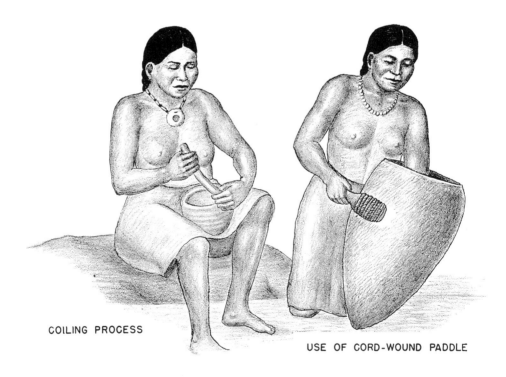

COILING PROCESS

USE OF CORD-WOUND PADDLE

burning in the midst of the blaze. After several hours of burning, the vessel reached a stage of almost white heat which produced a chemical change in the composition of the clay. Pottery making —the transformation of formless clay into an enduring substance —was one of man's earliest successful experiments in effecting chemical change.

Because of its durability, pottery furnishes one of archaeology's most useful research materials. Even the broken pieces, called potsherds, help to identify cultures. Pottery reveals technical

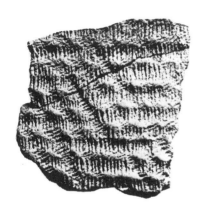

POTSHERDS SHOWING FABRIC AND CORD IMPRESSIONS

knowledge and artistic ideas of a people through the details of
its manufacture, shape and decoration. Moreover, the unlimited
plasticity of the clay permits expression of the potter's individuality as well as the traditions of the group. Thus, when it is
fired, it retains indefinitely the work of human hands and the
artistic ideas of human minds.

Although the earliest Woodland pottery bore on its surface the
imprints of cords or coarsely woven fabrics, some of the later
bore impressions made by carvings on wooden paddles. Pottery
with its surface decorated in this manner is called "stamped."
At first, the carvings were simple—merely parallel grooves, or
criss-crossed grooves—but as time went on, the designs became

POTSHERDS SHOWING STAMPED IMPRESSIONS OF CARVED PADDLE

more elaborate. The peak of artistic development in this method of decoration produced some of the most beautiful prehistoric Indian pottery. The stamping technique of decoration, which began in early Woodland times, continued as an artistic tradition in the Southeast until the nineteenth century when it was still practiced by the Cherokee. Undoubtedly, the early Woodland Indians of Tennessee borrowed the stamping idea from neighboring peoples in Georgia, since that area seems to have been the center of its development. Although travel in prehistoric times was arduous—on foot or in dugout canoes—contacts between tribes were frequent enough for ideas and techniques to spread widely.

Pottery was not the only material used for containers; steatite, often called soapstone, was available in the mountains. This soft stone was easily shaped into bowls with flint blades, and was also carved into various ornaments and "medicine tubes." The latter, biconical in shape, were instruments used by medicine

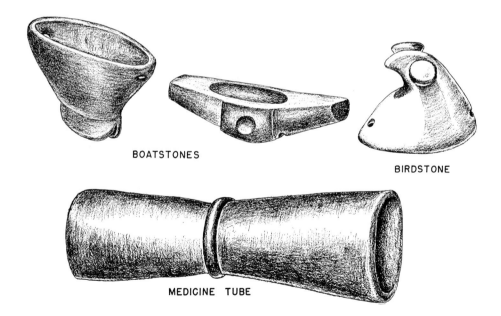

BOATSTONES

BIRDSTONE

MEDICINE TUBE

men. The custom of sucking or blowing through tubes was a medical procedure widely practiced by primitive Indian doctors. Through the tubes, they pretended to suck out diseases from ailing parts of the body. Other curious objects, usually carved from steatite, were small containers known as "boatstones" because of their shape. These apparently were worn suspended from the neck, since they always have holes at both ends, as well as grooved keels at the bottom. While their use and significance is unknown, their infrequent occurrence suggests that they, too, may have been accessories of the medicine men.

From thick green slate obtained in the mountains, tools and weapons as well as ornaments were made. Early Woodland axes usually had blades made from the green slate. These triangular blades, called celts, had pointed polls which in battle were just as lethal as the sharp edges. Axe blades, grooved where the handle was attached, were less numerous, but were made in a great range of sizes, from a few inches up to a foot in length. All of these blades were made by the pecking and grinding method, but only the bit was well ground.

Spear-thrower weights, some identical to Archaic ones, and

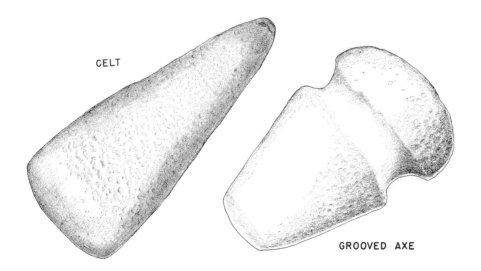

CELT

GROOVED AXE

others that had different shapes, were made from various attractive stones. The most common shape, a rectangular bar, was diagonally perforated at the ends. When such bars have conventionalized bird heads or tails carved at the ends, they are called "bird-stones." Other bird-stones depict only the bust portion of a bird with exaggerated pop-eyes.

While the spear-thrower was important, it was not the most effective weapon used by the early Woodland Indians, for they also had the bow and arrow. Whatever doubts about their use of the bow and arrow that may have existed at one time were dispelled in 1956. The discovery of a section of a two-thousand-year-old arrowshaft in a site in Greene County, Tennessee, settled the question. Although only eight and a half inches long, the cane arrowshaft section was the nock end. The cane, known as "switch cane," is a slender, tough variety that grows in uplands. It was used for arrowshafts by the historic Cherokee who called it *guni* (goonée)—the same word that they used for "arrow."

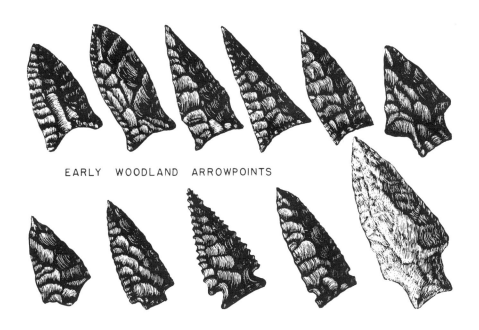

EARLY WOODLAND ARROWPOINTS

The nock in the prehistoric example was made just beyond a
joint; this prevented the shaft from splitting when the bow string
was drawn taut. By a fortunate accident the short section of cane
had been charred in some ancient fire. This accounted for its
preservation, for wood that has been carbonized resists decay.
Lying undisturbed five feet below the surface of the ground for
more than twenty centuries, this unprepossessing fragment of
charcoal became an important archaeological clue when it was
carefully unearthed in 1956 by an amateur archaeologist. It
proved beyond doubt that the early Woodland Indians used
the bow and arrow. The flint points that tipped the arrows varied
in details, but the most characteristic ones were triangular in
shape with either straight, incurved or excurved edges. Arrows,
tipped with these small, wickedly sharp points, were deadly
weapons capable of killing men and animals. Other types of
points with various stems and notches were used both on arrows
and spears, but the ones used on spears were usually larger.
Among the spearpoints, some were chipped from quartzite. This
hard, crystalline rock, which occurs in a range of colors—milky-
white, yellow, dove-gray, and pink—required much skill to shape.
The Indians evidently chose it for its beauty, since flint was
far easier to chip.

Flint tools, drills, knives and scrapers, differing only slightly
from those that had been used ever since Paleo-Indian times,
served the same purposes among the Woodland peoples. This
was true of most of the bone and antler tools which were indis-
tinguishable from those of the Archaic Indians. However, some
things differed, and among these was a curious form of antler
handle which was perforated from two sides and in some cases
decorated with engraving. The handle was apparently used on a
wooden implement, possibly a spear-thrower, to which it was
attached by an obliquely inserted wooden pin. Antler and bone,
decorated with carving and engraving, were used for ornaments
as well as tools. Large engraved antler combs that resemble the
ones worn in the hair by Spanish women may have served the

same purpose among Woodland women. On the other hand, combs are sometimes used in hand weaving to tighten the weft strands. By shape alone, the use of objects cannot always be determined.

But some things are unquestionably what they appear to be, as for example, necklaces. Strings of animal teeth for necklaces appealed particularly to the Woodland people. The teeth used most frequently came from bears, but bobcat, groundhog, elk, dog, and even human teeth were combined with them. On some of the more elaborate necklaces the teeth alternated with marine shell beads which came from the Gulf of Mexico. Tiny *olivellas* and *marginellas,* to be sewn on garments or strung for necklaces, were brought in by the thousands. Large conchs, too, were imported and cut up for beads and pendants. Beads were usually

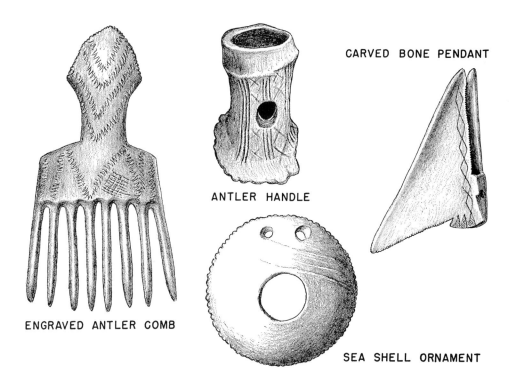

CARVED BONE PENDANT

ANTLER HANDLE

ENGRAVED ANTLER COMB

SEA SHELL ORNAMENT

shaped like flat disks, but some were inch-long tubes whose perforations represent remarkable skill with a very small drill. Skill in the use of flint cutting tools was also necessary to carve ring-shaped pendants, decorated with minutely scalloped edges.

Copper, either from the Lake Superior area or local deposits, was the rarest of the materials used for ornaments and was probably the most highly prized because of its scarcity. Its only use was for small beads that added bright accents to necklaces of white shell beads.

While the refuse of daily living—broken pots and tools, burned houses and garbage—that accumulated upon their old village sites provides a partial picture of the Woodland Indians' culture, very little would be known about their costumes and adornment without the knowledge gained from their graves. There were no special cemeteries in the villages; the graves were dug near the huts and were small, circular pits, not over two feet deep. In order to fit into such a small shallow grave, the corpse, with its arms and legs folded against the body, was tightly wrapped in mats or skins. These shapeless bundles were placed in the graves with the body lying in various positions—on its side, back, face, or even sitting up. Death in the form of disease or enemies sometimes struck suddenly and wiped out an entire family who were then buried in a single grave. One such burial included thirteen skeletons of men, women and children. The skeletons sometimes show unmistakable signs of violence—arrowpoints embedded in the bones, skulls bashed in by tomahawks, and broken or mutilated limbs.

In death as well as in life, these Indians wore red ochre paint made from hematite, an iron ore that was ground into powder and mixed with grease or water. Traces of body paint often stain the bones of the skeletons, and sometimes a mass of the powdered paint appears to have been scattered over the corpse. The color of red ochre so closely resembles the color of fresh blood that most primitive peoples have attributed magical powers to it. Besides using it for body and face paint, the Indians generally employed it for decorating all sorts of objects.

The skeletons reveal little difference in appearance between the early Woodland and Archaic Indians. The reason for this is the common Asiatic ancestry of both populations. Both belonged to the same racial stock, the American Indian, which includes eight or more distinguishable varieties. None of these is exclusively associated with any particular culture, and most of them share several features, such as straight, black hair and broad cheekbones. These traits are shared also by the Asiatic or Mongoloid division of mankind. A few, especially some of the older types, because of narrower faces and high-bridged prominent noses, resemble more the white or Caucasoid division. Yet in the distant past, just as at present, local populations were always somewhat variable, even when a majority of the individuals belonged to a particular type.

Four thousand years ago is a conservative date to set for the appearance of the Woodland Indians in the southeastern United States, because a site on the Georgia coast in which pottery was found is dated nearly that early by radiocarbon. In Tennessee, the only radiocarbon date so far for a site of the Woodland Indians is about 100 B.C. However, this by no means dates their arrival, for by that time they had long been established in the area. Their knowledge of the country and its resources, as shown by their use of materials coming from various parts of the Southeast, is proof of that. The Tennessee radiocarbon date came from a site at the junction of Camp Creek with the Nolichucky River in Greene County, a site which represents one of the early phases of the Woodland culture—the Camp Creek phase. Another, and slightly later, is the Candy Creek phase during which contacts with Georgia Indians, friendly or otherwise, introduced the technique of stamped decoration on pottery to groups along the Hiwassee River. At the Candy Creek site in Bradley County, sherds from pottery actually made by Georgia Indians were found in refuse pits, mixed with others from locally made pottery with similar designs, but distinguishable by the nature of the ware. The Georgia ware which contained sand had a smooth, fine texture, while the Candy Creek ware, to which ground limestone particles had been added, had a coarser texture.

Borrowing ideas from their neighbors in this manner, the early Woodland Indians gradually modified their traditional ways of life as they spread throughout the Southland. In a yet unknown locality, some of them came in contact with peoples whose ideas so influenced their own that they began to devote much of their time and energy to new interests. This was to result in the creation of Tennessee's first permanent monuments—the burial mounds that are found throughout the State—and to usher in the fourth era of Stone Age culture.

Chapter 4

Burial Mound Builders

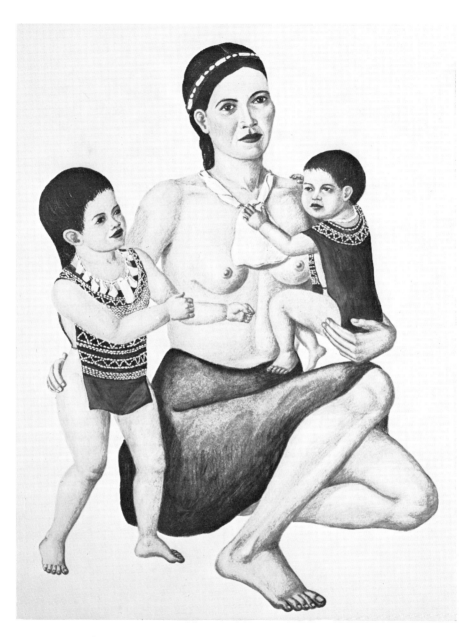

WOMAN AND CHILDREN WEARING SEA SHELL ORNAMENTS

Burial Mound Builders

Centuries before Alexander the Great conquered the civilized world in 330 B.C., even before the Roman Republic was born on the hills of Latium in 500 B.C., an exotic Woodland culture was developing in the primeval forests of America. Although it was rooted in the same tradition as other Woodland cultures, it far out-distanced them in esthetic, social and ceremonial growth. Its dominant themes were solicitude for the dead and preparation for life after death. Consequently, the richest treasures of the tribe were consigned to the tombs, and great earthen mounds— intended as everlasting monuments—were built over the tombs.

The idea of erecting burial mounds spread far and wide among peoples who lived in the eastern woodlands. Some tribes elaborated upon the idea by developing complicated rituals and building large groups of architectural earthworks, while others never went beyond a relatively simple concept. However, regardless of where burial mounds were built, a death cult—imbued with doctrines of souls, ghosts and a life hereafter—was the incentive. This death cult had its most highly developed expression among peoples who were separated from each other by great distances. In fact, the cult may have originated in some region far beyond the eastern woodlands.

In the highlands of Guatemala near the western edge of a

broad valley, there is a place known as Kaminaljuyu, "Hills of the
Dead," where more than two hundred mounds, once founda-
tions for buildings, often enclosed fabulous tombs. Each tomb, a
large chamber timbered with logs, held the record of a poten-
tate's funeral. Adorned with ornaments of jade—the people's
rarest and most precious substance—as well as with jaguar jaws,
pearls, shell beads and pendants, the principal personage occupied the center of the tomb. Around him were placed the
remains of sacrificial victims who were to be his servants in the
hereafter. In addition, there were engraved trophy skulls and
other objects made from human bones which implied human
sacrifice.

The civilization of the people of Kaminaljuyu was one in which
great ceremonial capitals were the centers for all major religions
and political activities. Like other cultures in Mexico and South
America, it was a mature flowering of an old formative tradition
out of which also stemmed lesser growths in the eastern woodlands.

In the Ohio Valley before the beginning of the Christian era,
a people known as the Hopewellians built the most impressive
burial mounds in the New World—one of the largest being five
hundred feet long and higher than a two-story building. Earthen
embankments formed immense geometrical enclosures covering
as much as a hundred acres within which the burial mounds
were arranged. Log tombs within the mounds, like those at
Kaminaljuyu, held the remains of important personages, who
also were often accompanied by sacrificial victims and skulls.
Sometimes the bodies had been cremated, but in all cases the
tombs contained the treasured possessions of the deceased.

From far and wide the Hopewellian Indians secured precious
substances—conch shells from the Gulf, pearls from the rivers,
obsidian from the Rockies, mica from the Appalachians, copper
from the Lake Superior region, and silver from no one knows
where. Skilled hands fashioned these and other materials into
exquisite ornaments, elaborate headdresses, breastplates, weapons

and sculptured tobacco pipes.

The elegance and artistic achievements of Hopewellian culture rested upon the firm foundation of corn agriculture. The corn variety was undoubtedly the eastern flint type widely grown by Indians of eastern America, and still raised by some American farmers. It was a slender, flexible cob with eight rows of kernels and is one of the varieties that is found in the highlands of Guatemala, both in prehistoric sites and in today's fields. Although highland Guatemala is not a large geographical area, it has more varieties of corn than almost any other single region. The prehistoric types that originated there spread far into North America and became the ancestors of the modern corn belt varieties. With its tall, vigorous plants and heavy yield, corn became not only the sustainer of many American Indian groups, but also the central theme of their ceremonial life.

How did a Guatemala type of corn happen to be grown by the Hopewellians? Most likely it was passed from tribe to tribe, and perhaps mounds, tombs, trophy skulls and the rest of the death cult spread the same way. The similarities between the Kaminaljuyu culture of Guatemala and that of the Hopewellians of the United States could have been due to diffusion of plants and ideas northward. But, they could just as well have been parallel developments out of a basic formative pattern.

Most regions had their own cultural individuality during the burial mound era, but all were interrelated to some extent. The tribes in the southern region had much in common with peoples elsewhere. They exchanged goods of many kinds and borrowed ideas from each other. A network of trails criss-crossed the forests, serving as channels for the spread of farming, fashions, mounds and rituals. In the Tennessee region, the compact little villages of the early Woodland Indians were not exempt from such outside influences.

Outposts of Hopewellian-type culture existed in the South, along the Gulf coast and scattered here and there inland, even as far west as eastern Oklahoma. All or most of the North American burial mound cultures appear to stem from the basic Woodland pattern. But in the Ohio Valley it had its most vigorous and elaborated development. That region seems to have been a center from which influences dispersed to Tennessee. Even the early Woodland Indians, living on Camp Creek in the remote foothills of the Smoky Mountains, had rare objects like the "pop-eyed" bird-stone whose inspiration was Hopewellian.

Perhaps it was the dramatic pageantry of Hopewellian funeral ceremonies that appealed so strongly to other Woodland Indians that in time they, too, adopted the building of burial mounds. From the towering earthworks of the Hopewellians to the simple, dome-shaped mounds of most of the Tennessee Woodland Indians was a far cry. Yet the same idea was present—lasting, visible memorials to the dead.

The burial mounds of eastern Tennessee were small, seldom

BURIAL MOUND IN MEIGS COUNTY, TENNESSEE

exceeding fifty feet in diameter and ten feet in height, yet they often contained more than a hundred graves. In the core of each mound, either sunk into a pit below the surface of the ground, or built on the surface, a special grave was constructed. Sometimes it was a small log tomb, crudely made, but nevertheless the counterpart of Hopewellian and Kaminaljuyu tombs. Logs were laid along the sides and over the corpse, and then earth was piled over the whole to form a small mound that became the core of the eventual larger one. The occasion for starting a new mound may have been the death of a chief or clan leader. In any event, the first interment was the only one to be accorded such treatment, because the later burials were placed on the ground surface, either beside or on top of the initial one. There were no graves in the usual sense because the bodies were merely covered with earth. At times, a layer of clam shells enclosed the body, a custom confined mainly to eastern Tennessee.

Trophy skulls, too, were buried in the mounds, and evidence of violent death was common. Headless, handless and otherwise mutilated skeletons have been found. Many warriors, as well as women and children, were killed by arrows whose flint points had shattered bones or lodged in vital organs. Whether the violent deaths signify murder, battle, or sacrifice is unknown. The dust of centuries has long since obscured the full meaning of events that are only partly revealed by archaeology.

A large tomb, uncovered in Rhea County, Tennessee, was contained in one mound of a group located on a small elevation near the Tennessee River bank. The mound enclosing the tomb was eleven feet high, oval in shape, and had a length of sixty feet. The tomb itself, a cribbing of large logs, was twelve feet long and eight feet wide. Two bodies had been laid side by side on the earthen floor of the tomb, and around the bodies were numerous objects to accompany the spirits of the dead on their last journey—stone celts, arrowpoints, bone tools and pottery vessels. Logs, a foot in diameter, formed the roof of the tomb which was partly burned during the funeral ceremony. Before

the tomb and its contents were completely consumed, the building of the mound commenced. Basket loads of earth, heaped
over the smouldering remains, caused the structure to collapse.

In eastern Tennessee, the burial mound builders are called
Hamilton Indians, named from Hamilton County where their
culture is well represented. Although they had ceremonial burial
centers represented by groups of mounds, they lived in straggling
settlements that extended a mile or more along the river bank.
Each family had its individual homestead widely separated from
those of its nearest neighbors. Their dwellings, probably built of
small saplings, have left no traces; only refuse piles mark the
approximate locations today. The refuse, mainly an accumulation of clam shells, shows that the lowly mussel furnished a large
part of the food supply.

So little of anything has lasted in the old village sites and
mounds that the life of the people seems much poorer than in-
deed it was. All of the things made of bark and wood, of leather,
fibers and feathers have decayed. Gone also are the songs, the
drums, the rattles and flutes, and the rhythm of dancing feet.
But, the indestructible objects of stone, shell and pottery have
survived in the mounds and trash heaps to reveal at least part
of the people's daily life.

Tools, weapons and pottery differed only slightly from those
of the earlier Woodland Indians. The small, triangular arrow-

TRIANGULAR ARROWPOINTS

point was gradually refined into a needle-sharp messenger of death to man and beast alike. The old cord and fabric-marked pottery gave way to smoother surfaces. Stamped decoration was gradually abandoned, to be replaced by incised and punctated designs. Except for the large cooking pots which continued to have conical bottoms, the vessels became shallower and hemispherical in shape. Yet, crushed limestone was still added to the clay, just as in early Woodland times.

Ornaments differed somewhat in style. The most unique —highly popular with both sexes—were massive, spirally shaped shell beads. Weighing from a quarter to half a pound, they varied in length from six to nine inches and were drilled from end to end. The drilling was done with a tiny flint bit, less than an

NECKLACES MADE FROM SEA SHELLS

eighth of an inch thick and about an inch long, which was fastened to a slender reed. It was truly a feat of fine craftsmanship to have been performed with a primitive tool. With the drilling proceeding half way from each end, great precision was required to make the two borings meet. These beads were so long that only three or four were quite enough for a necklace, and when a large shell pendant was also added, the necklace was a ponderous affair. When several more of the spiral beads were attached to the arms, as was often the case, the jewelry probably outweighed all the rest of the Indian's costume. These beads did not entirely replace the older kinds of shell and stone ornaments worn in early Woodland times. They were apparently an innovation of such spectacular nature that they caught the popular fancy.

The tobacco pipe of familiar shape made its first appearance in the burial mound era. Some of the Woodland pipes were the models for the shape of those in use today. While elaborate variations were made by some tribes, the Hamilton Indians of eastern Tennessee were satisfied with simple shapes that had almost no decoration. Their pipes were made of steatite or pottery and are often found with the carbonized "cake" from burned tobacco still preserved in the bowls.

Tobacco was used throughout most of the New World, either chewed, snuffed or smoked, depending upon local custom. The effect of the nicotine was about the same, regardless of how it was taken. The smoking of tobacco by the American Indians was mainly for magical and religious purposes, and only secondarily for pastime. Among the historic southern Indians, wild tobacco, *Nicotiana rustica,* was a carefully tended plant, and its flowers as well as its leaves were used in rituals. During councils, ceremonial pipe smoking formed an integral part of the formalities; it was a pledge to bind peace treaties and a rite to invoke the high gods. Similar customs which involved pipe smoking as a symbolic act were so widely observed by American Indians that they must have originated almost as long ago as the use of tobacco itself.

The Hamilton Indians were only one among several groups that inhabited Tennessee during the burial mound era. From the eastern part of the State where they lived, the Tennessee River swings southwestward in a great arc through Alabama. Then, reversing its original direction, it flows northward to join the Ohio. The great winding valley, well over a thousand miles long, was a natural communication and transportation route in prehistoric times. Although, for the most part a tranquil stream, in its great arc through Alabama it followed a serpentine course through numerous ridges where it swept over rapids and shoals.

TOBACCO PIPES CARVED FROM STONE

This section of the river with its stretches of swift, shallow water formed a province that was somewhat of an impediment to canoe travel between the upper and lower portions of the valley. Its existence may partly explain why cultural differences existed in the three main divisions of the valley throughout most of the prehistoric period. During the burial mound era, while the Hamilton Indians lived along the quiet upper reaches, another

HAMILTON INDIAN MAN

group inhabited the shoals and rapids section of the river's great arc in Alabama; still others lived on the shores of the tranquil lower portion in western Tennessee.

The culture of the people who lived in the middle portion is called "Copena," a word coined from "copper" and "galena"—two minerals frequently found with burials in that area. The typical graves in Copena mounds were basin-shaped vaults, lined with puddled clay (clay mixed with water), and equipped with head and foot rests, made also from puddled clay. The covers from such vaults were made of bark slabs or logs, over which clay was spread. After a group of clay tombs had accumulated, they were covered with earth to form a low mound. Then more burials were added, either in clay tombs or merely covered with earth. Cremation, which was occasionally practiced, took place either in the clay basins or elsewhere; if the latter were the case, the ashes were gathered up and buried in the mounds.

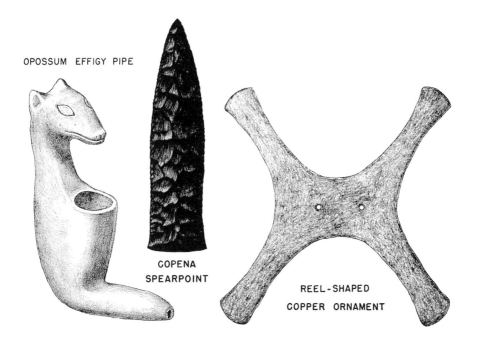

OPOSSUM EFFIGY PIPE

COPENA
SPEARPOINT

REEL-SHAPED
COPPER ORNAMENT

Copper objects are particularly abundant in Copena mounds; moreover, they occur in a greater variety of forms than were used by earlier peoples. In addition to beads, the metal was wrought into breastplates, reel-shaped gorgets, bracelets, ear ornaments and ceremonial axe blades. Evidently, the Copena people preferred copper ornaments in contrast to the Hamilton Indians' preference for shell. The other substance that was highly prized by the Copena people is galena, a lead ore that occurs in the form of lead-gray crystals. It may have been valued for its glittering beauty alone, since it is found merely as lumps in the graves. However, such lumps, often facetted from grinding, may have yielded a sparkling powder to be used for ornamentation.

Copena spearpoints were distinctive in shape, quite different from those of neighboring peoples. Greenstone celts were noteworthy especially for their graceful form, but also for their unusual length and highly polished finish. All in all, the Copena culture appears to have been technically more advanced than the Hamilton, and reflects closer relationships to the Hopewellian.

Passing downstream from the Copena province, the burial mound culture had still another expression in western Tennessee. While small, conical mounds were numerous there, more elaborate earthworks were also constructed. The people responsible for the latter are known as the Harmon's Creek Indians, from one of their village sites at the mouth of Harmon's Creek in Benton County, Tennessee.

The most spectacular of their ceremonial centers was in Stewart County on a high ridge that rises abruptly about two hundred feet above the valley floor. The ridge, overshadowing the village that lay at its foot along the river, was crowned with terraces and mounds. The uppermost terrace was entirely constructed by human labor, the crest of the ridge having been leveled off first and then the edges banked up. Two projecting spurs of the ridge formed the lower terraces, which had also been leveled and banked. Mounds were built on all of the terraces, but it was the summit that dominated the scene.

Many centuries ago, the Harmon's Creek people had conducted their elaborate funeral ceremonies on the spot. They had paved a large oblong area with small rocks and near one corner had built a chamber for their dead. This chamber, constructed of saplings and plastered over with clay, had also been banked around the outside with small rocks to a height of five feet and several feet in thickness. The chamber was literally a "bone house." For inside, on shelves and platforms, baskets containing the bones of the dead had been placed. At some time in the distant past, the bone house had been destroyed by fire and a large oblong mound built over its remains and the adjacent pavement. The smaller mounds on the lower terraces held a similar story.

The burial customs revealed by these Harmon's Creek mounds resemble very much those of the historic Choctaws. Although it is unlikely that the Harmon's Creek Indians were ancestors of the Choctaws, we may draw upon eye-witness accounts of Choctaw culture to gain greater understanding of the prehistoric remains.

Among the Choctaws, every village and sometimes individual families had their own bone houses. But there were always special centers where the remains of the chiefs were preserved. Such centers were also headquarters for the "buzzard men" or "bone gatherers," highly respected elders who performed the task of cleaning and packing the bones.

It was the custom at the death of a person to build a high scaffold on which the body was kept for four or five months. Covered with skins and bark, and furnished with food, drink, weapons and an extra pair of moccasins, the dead rested in state until the spirit was believed to have been released from the body. The scaffold was concealed by a palisade of poles, outside of which the mourners performed the death rites. Each morning the women relatives of the dead, weeping and moaning, would circle slowly around the palisade. Men mourned during the darkness of night, possibly to conceal their grief.

After four or five months, when the flesh of the dead body had decomposed, the family sent for the "buzzard man." He was an aged man, tattooed and painted in a special manner to denote his office. On both hands, he had long, talon-like nails on the thumb and first two fingers. It was his task, using only his long fingernails, to scrape off the last vestiges of flesh from the bones. Then he placed the bones in a wooden or woven cane chest which he deposited in the "bone house." Meanwhile, the scaffold and palisade were burned. The last rite was a funeral feast, over which the "buzzard man" presided.

Each year two memorial ceremonies were held, one in the

MOURNING THE DEAD AT THE "CRY POLE"

spring and another in the fall. They were the great "feast of souls" or "cries of the kindred" that were performed to reassure the dead—whose spirits were supposed to hover nearby—that their bones were properly cared for. During these ceremonies, the bone chests were brought out and piled up around a "cry pole," a tall post erected for the purpose. For two days and nights, the piercing wails of the relatives continuously rent the air. Then, after everybody had had a good cry, the chests were replaced in the bone house, and the feast which followed soon assuaged the grief.

When the bone houses became filled, and the chests and houses themselves began to decay, they were enclosed in mounds. Sometimes they were set afire and mostly consumed before the mounds were built.

The rock-walled chamber of the Harmon's Creek Indians, previously described, was one of these bone houses that had been destroyed by fire, either intentionally or accidentally, since it contained twenty-one badly charred bundles of bones. The adjacent oblong pavement was possibly the place where bone chests were stacked near a cry pole during the "feasts of souls." Certainly, the whole ridge top had been dedicated to ceremonies of a death cult. In time, the original bone house and pavement were buried beneath a large platform mound, over a hundred feet long, sixty feet wide, and ten feet high. Built against one of the longer sides was a ramp that led to the summit. When ceremonies were performed they would have been fully visible to people assembled on the surrounding lower terraces.

This large earthwork foreshadowed another era of mound building, an era that began with the advent of new peoples, and ended only when white conquest destroyed forever the native American civilizations. The new peoples were the vanguard of a large group of tribes that were soon to dominate the southeastern scene. From them the burial mound Indians learned new ways, as they mingled peacefully in some places and offered resistance in others. Some of the Woodland Indians may have abandoned their settlements and moved northward to the Ohio Valley, since that region was the home of the tribe known as the Shawnee, whose name in their own language means "Southerners."

Although the burial mound era ended centuries before Columbus, the Woodland Indians left their permanent mark upon the Tennessee region in the form of hundreds of earthworks and abandoned village sites. Furthermore, they had a substantial influence upon those tribes that supplanted and absorbed them, for elements of their ceremonialism can be recognized in the culture of their successors.

Chapter 5

The Age of
Temple Mounds

TEMPLE MOUND ON HIWASSEE ISLAND

The Age of Temple Mounds

Still majestic in decay stand the great temple mounds. The temples that once crowned their heights, like the hands that built them, have long since crumbled to dust. And their contours, blurred by the centuries' winds and rains, erode a little more each day.

A thousand years before Columbus, the age of temple mounds began in the South. From the Gulf of Mexico northward, throughout most of the Mississippi Valley and the Southeast, a dynamic cultural tradition spread. It embodied ceremonial and political concepts that were more advanced than those of the earlier cultures. Although tribes continued to exist as major language groupings, the vital social and political units were towns, provinces and confederacies.

The new tradition that appeared is often called the "Mississippian" culture because much of it was concentrated in the river valley of the same name. The Mississippian Indians were, in reality, many tribes speaking different tongues, but most of them belonged to two large language families, the Caddoan to the west of the Mississippi River and the Muskhogean to the east. Later on, many other tribes besides those belonging to these two language groups adopted the new way of life. Thus, when referring to Mississippian peoples, they are defined as those who shared a similar culture, regardless of what tribe or nation they belonged to, or what language they spoke. But, above all, most of them built temple mounds.

No one has yet been able to trace the Muskhogeans or Caddoans back to a definite place of origin. However, the traditions of the Muskhogean-speaking Indians contain legends of their migrations from some unknown, earlier homeland west of the Mississippi River. They were a numerous people divided into many tribes that spread rapidly over the Southeast. Appropriating the most desirable locations, from which they often evicted the Woodland peoples, they became the dominant southern Indian nations.

In the search for the origin of the new cultural tradition, the closest resemblances can be found far south in Middle America where temple mounds originated. The great centers of civilization in the Valley of Mexico, Guatemala and Yucatan were flourishing long before the Mississippian tradition developed. In the magnificent art and architecture, and in the complex rituals of Middle America, were elements that can be recognized in Mississippian cultures, although their expression was more primitive. Such elements may have traveled by diffusion from tribe to tribe, but it is more probable that the ancestral Muskhogeans and other Mississippian tribes originally lived on the peripheries of the Middle American civilizations. If such were true, as marginal peoples they shared the basic ideas, yet failed to develop them to the same degree of excellence.

Very few, if any, areas of the world have shown continuous cultural evolution without the addition of new populations, as well as the borrowing of culture traits. At times the local populations were almost entirely replaced. In the Tigris-Euphrates Valley, the ancient civilization of the Sumerians was superseded by that of the Semitic Babylonians, which in turn fell to the Persians. The Nile Valley during the dynastic period of Egyptian history was subject to successive invasions by Hyksos, Nubians, Persians and Greeks. Greece was invaded by Hellenes, Minoans,

Thracians, Phrygians and Dorians, each contributing to its civilization. The Etruscans, who migrated from some part of Asia Minor into Italy, bequeathed their culture to the Italici, thus giving birth to Roman civilization. England, overwhelmed time and again by invasions from the continent of Europe, owed its Bronze Age to a nameless invading group, its Iron Age to the Kelts, its language to Anglo-Saxons, and its civilization to the Romans and Normans. The Valley of Mexico, under migrant tribes and foreign influences, became one of the great centers of classic civilizations in the New World.

Consequently, the temple mound age north of the Rio Grande seems to reflect a widespread movement of peoples who brought with them a Middle American tradition. This tradition was reflected in the ceremonial centers, with their plazas and temple mounds that were the foci of Mississippian Indian life. Arts and crafts also reveal similarities. And, among the rituals and beliefs of the historic Muskhogean tribes can be traced elements comparable to those of Middle America.

While the flat-topped temple pyramids of Middle America were plated with either cut stone or cement over rubble cores, those of the Mississippian Indians were built wholly of earth. Yet they were alike in general shape and in having been built in stages. In both regions the temples were used for religious ceremonies, but the Mississippian ones also served for other affairs— council chambers in which civil affairs were conducted, wars declared, and peace treaties consummated. In fact, the political and religious functions were often closely related.

The first stage in the construction of a Mississippian temple mound began with the demolishing of an outworn council chamber and the covering of its remains with earth. The low, flat-topped pyramid that resulted then became the foundation for a new temple, or temples, since in some cases two structures were built side by side on the summit. The same foundation was sometimes used for a successive series of buildings without the addition of earth. Since the buildings were constructed of wood,

Courtesy of Museo Nacional de Antropologia, Mexico, D. F.

MIDDLE AMERICAN TEMPLE PYRAMIDS—THE CASTILLO AT CHICHEN ITZA, YUCATAN (UPPER), AND
PYRAMID OF THE SUN AT TEOTIHUACAN, MEXICO (LOWER)

cane and thatch, they were easily ignited by accident, and had a limited duration at best. Undoubtedly, fires destroyed some, while others were razed when their frameworks weakened. As additions were made to the mounds, their heights increased, reaching elevations of nearly one hundred feet in some exceptional instances.

The temple pyramids in Mexico were similarly rebuilt and enlarged, but there the reconstruction took place in accordance with a regular calendrical cycle of fifty-two years. Fortunately, when the Spaniards conquered Mexico, the traditional history and customs of the Aztecs were recorded for posterity. It is known that the periodic renovations formed part of one of the most solemn Aztec ceremonies, a ceremony that recurred every fifty-two years. Called the New Fire Ceremony, the sacred fire, regarded as the symbol of life which had been kept perpetually burning, was extinguished and rekindled. The fifty-two-year cycle was derived from a combination of the Aztec sun calendar of 365 days and eighteen "months" of twenty days each plus five extra days, and of a ritual calendar of 260 days with twenty "weeks" of thirteen days each. During the last five days of the final year of a fifty-two-year cycle, the sacred fire that burned on an altar in the temple and all of the household fires in the nation were extinguished. Household furnishings were destroyed, temples were razed, and the people fasted.

On the evening of the last day, priests gathered in a temple on the summit of an extinct volcano called the Hill of the Star. When a particular star reached the center of the sky, the sacred fire was rekindled by the priests in the open breast of a sacrificial victim. Torches lighted from the new fire were carried by runners to the temple altars of every town throughout the empire. The hearth fires of all the homes were in turn relighted from the altar flames, and life was thus symbolically renewed for another cycle.

Whether any sort of cycle was involved in the rebuilding of the Mississippian temple mounds is unknown. Nothing in the ceremonial life of the historic Muskhogean tribes gives any clue, nor is there any evidence of a system of recording events over long periods which would be necessary for an extended cycle.

So far, the earliest dated Mississippian temple mound is located in eastern Texas. Radiocarbon dating places it in the fifth century A.D. Other mounds in Louisiana and Illinois are dated as late as the twelfth and fourteenth centuries. Sometime within this span of eight hundred years such mounds appeared in the Tennessee Valley.

Throughout the western part of Tennessee, temple mound sites are numerous along the Mississippi River and its small tributary streams. These include the Wolf, Hatchie, Forked Deer, and Obion rivers. A large ceremonial center, far up the southern branch of the Forked Deer River near the village of Pinson, includes among many others one mound that towers to the height of seventy feet. On the southern outskirts of Memphis, another important center, called Chucalissa, is located.

One of the most impressive, covering more than twenty-five acres, is on the headwaters of the Obion River in Henry County. Its spacious plaza, a thousand feet long and five hundred wide, is flanked by five mounds. The largest is an immense pyramidal earthwork approached by a broad ramp leading to the summit. Including the ramp, it is nearly five hundred feet long and one hundred and seventy feet broad. Although only thirty feet in height, it was built on high, level ground above the flood plain and dominated the surrounding countryside. Its great bulk represented six stages of construction, each succeeding addition increasing the dimensions. Excavations have revealed that this ceremonial center was established early in the temple mound period.

In the western valley of the Tennessee River are more temple mound sites. Near Savannah, where the battle of Shiloh was fought during the Civil War, the remains of a remarkable fortified city lie along a bluff sixty feet high. Two lines of fortifications enclose it, except on the river side. The outer wall, nearly a mile and a quarter long, has bastions projecting outward for forty feet and spaced two hundred and fifty feet apart. The inner wall parallels the outer at a distance of one hundred and fifty feet, and also has bastions which are staggered with those of the outer wall. These fortifications which remain today as earthen embankments were once topped with log palisades. A large temple mound occupies the center of the enclosure, with fifteen smaller earthworks distributed on either side.

Middle Tennessee has its temple mound sites in the valley of the Cumberland River. Where the Harpeth River, a branch of the Cumberland, makes two adjacent bends, lies one of the most spectacular of all ancient sites in Tennessee. It has two divisions, one of which is on high ground, protected on the river side by precipitous bluffs and on the other side by defense works like those at Shiloh. The entire hill top had been leveled off and terraced, creating a plaza about a thousand feet long and five hundred feet wide. One large temple mound and two smaller ones had been built near the edge overlooking the river bottom. On a terrace below the plaza, two more mounds had been constructed. The entire area enclosed by the fortification is over three hundred acres. Less than a mile away, where the river makes a deep loop, lies the other division of the site. Almost completely surrounded by the river, except for a narrow neck, it occupies level bottom land. There, another broad plaza with one enormous temple mound and a number of smaller ones had formed a second ceremonial center. If, as seems likely, this was a single large town composed of the two widely separated divisions, its population must have been very large. In fact, the whole Central Basin area of Middle Tennessee had a dense population during the temple mound period.

The best known, although by no means the largest, temple mound sites in Tennessee are in the eastern part of the State. From Chattanooga northeastward into the remote valleys of the headwaters of the Tennessee River, flowed the tide of Mississippian migrations. Medium-sized towns were established along

the Clinch, Powell, French Broad, Pigeon and Little Tennessee
rivers, as well as along the main Tennessee. Some were settled
early and became centers from which cultural influences radi-
ated. Others, settled much later, reflect the results of interaction
that took place between the Mississippian and Woodland peoples. In fact, it appears that many Woodland groups eventually
became incorporated with the newcomers. Partly because of this,
and for other reasons, it is possible to distinguish earlier and
later versions of Mississippian culture in eastern Tennessee and
elsewhere. Through excavation of many sites, the story of some
five hundred years of the temple mound age has been unfolded.

One site in particular, located on Hiwassee Island at the confluence of the Hiwassee River with the Tennessee, has furnished
a fairly complete picture of Mississippian life, including its early
period known as the Hiwassee Island phase. This phase began
sometime between the eleventh and twelfth centuries A.D. and
lasted perhaps two centuries.

Hiwassee Island, about seven hundred acres in extent, was
triangular in shape. When the Mississippian town was established at the head of the island, a plaza was laid out and the
first temple was built at one end. It was a small, oblong structure
covering less than a thousand square feet. Apparently built to
serve the immediate needs of a pioneering group, it was shortly
replaced by another almost twice its size. Both of these structures
were built on the original land surface. As the town grew larger,
even the second temple was no longer adequate for the activities
of such an important center. Thus it was disposed of, and three
new ones were built. They were arranged in a slight arc; at each
end was a large, oblong building and in the center a smaller one.
A small, flat-topped pyramid was built in front of the central
building, and another in front of one of the large temples; the
other large temple stood on a low earthen foundation. A palisade
surrounding the small building provided a concealed courtyard
for secret outdoor activities of the priests. Clay stairways gave
access to the tops of the small pyramids where chiefs or priests

could address the people or preside over ceremonies taking place on the plaza. During this period, the entire town, covering about ten acres, was enclosed by a palisade. Within this area, dwelling houses were clustered thickly about the plaza.

The first actual mound construction was a foundation four feet high that covered almost all of the area previously occupied by the three temples. Upon this, two new temples were erected, approached by a ramp in one instance and a clay stairway in the other. This general pattern was followed for two more stages of construction. Although neither stage added much to the height of the mound, the surface was completely renewed, stairways rebuilt, and the over-all size increased. The fourth addition was a massive one, raising the summit to a height of eleven feet above the plaza. After three more additions, the temples stood upon a

THREE EARLY TEMPLES ON HIWASSEE ISLAND

foundation twenty-two feet in height and covered nearly half
an acre. While the mound itself was only reconstructed seven
times, the temples were renewed sixteen times.

The seven successive renewals of the mound suggest some
recurrent time cycle, but the replacement of the perishable temples was dependent upon the uncertainties of destruction by fire
or deterioration from age. Including the pre-mound building
level, eight major stages of reconstruction of the ceremonial area
took place during the existence of the town. While it is possible
that such major construction enterprises were undertaken oftener
than twice in a century, it is unlikely. On that basis alone, four
hundred years would be represented by the eight stages. This
would place the founding of the town back in the thirteenth or
fourteenth century, depending upon when mound building
ceased. Since no records exist of mounds having been built in
Tennessee during the early eighteenth century, the period of
British colonial trade, 1700 A.D., may be taken as a terminal date.
It is most likely that the town was founded in the eleventh or
twelfth century. Whatever its actual duration in years, the town
on Hiwassee Island had a long history that covered most of the
temple mound age in Tennessee. The last half of this history
represented the later version of Mississippian culture, when many
changes in customs appeared.

Twenty miles downstream from Hiwassee Island was another
strategically located Mississippian town. There, Dallas Island,
which was a mile long, divided the stream into two channels. The
town during some periods occupied both sides of the river, as
well as the head of the island. This ancient metropolis, now submerged under Chickamauga Lake, had three large temple
mounds built during different periods.

The first settlement was on the east bank, opposite the center
of the island. On two pyramidal mounds, about twenty-five feet
apart, the first temples were erected. Later, the two mounds,
incorporated into a single unit, 230 feet long by 130 feet wide,
became the foundation for a large temple. Still later, the height

of one-half of the mound was increased by five feet, and eventually the rest was brought up to approximately the same level.

Meanwhile the town had expanded to the opposite side of the river where another ceremonial center was established. Here, as on Hiwassee Island, the first and second temples were built upon the original land surface. The first stage of mound construction on which three successive temples were built was four feet high. Later stages added nine more feet. During the period of the later additions, a third ceremonial center was developed across the river near the foot of the island.

This third development occurred during a time of transition between the early and late phases of the temple mound culture. Architecture was changing—the council chamber in the third ceremonial center was almost identical in details to those of the historic Creek Indians. The great prehistoric community, with its three ceremonial centers, has as long a history as the one on Hiwassee Island. These are but two among many others in eastern Tennessee that spanned the whole temple mound period. A very few of the towns were abandoned during the early half of the period, but a greater number were not established until the latter half. The increase in number of the late towns may have been due to expansion of population through the incorporation of Woodland Indian groups.

The arts, crafts and customs of the Hiwassee Island people were a more constant part of their daily life than the periodic construction of mounds. The manner in which they built their temples and dwelling houses is one activity that reveals their craftsmanship. The first step was to outline the floor area with narrow trenches about two feet deep. Next, long saplings, four or five inches in diameter, set upright and spaced about six inches apart, were set in the trenches which were then filled in and firmly tamped. Then, long, slender poles were bound horizontally to the uprights to stabilize them. The roof framework, a remarkable piece of construction, was woven like a huge basket. Most Indians were excellent basket makers, but these people went even further by actually weaving the roofs over their heads. The weaving process began at the corners, using the end poles of the walls. First, the two end poles from opposite walls were bent inward and their ends lashed together. This was repeated at the other ends of the same two walls. Then, the same was done with the end poles of the other two opposing walls and, as the weaving process continued alternating from side to side, all of the wall uprights became interwoven in an over-and-under pattern. As the work progressed, the roof assumed a dome shape. The result was an exceptionally sturdy type of roof construction, one that was able to withstand strong winds because it was actually a continuation of the walls.

A DWELLING CONSTRUCTED BY INTERWEAVING THE ROOF FRAMEWORK

When the framework was complete the exterior surfaces of the walls were lathed with split cane and plastered with clay. Then the roof was covered with grass thatching which partly overhung the walls to protect the clay plaster from the rains. Inside, finely woven cane mats covered the walls and floors, but were used more lavishly in temples than in dwelling houses.

The larger temples (averaging 35 by 55 feet) could accommodate up to three hundred persons without undue crowding. Some, however, were partitioned into two rooms, the back one serving for sacred rites or the storage of sacred objects, and only the front one providing space for councils and ceremonies. The temple entrance was its least conspicuous feature, being nothing more than a narrow gap at one corner. Inside, near the center of the floor, was always an altar, a circular or rectangular platform modeled from clay with a small central fire basin where the sacred fire burned perpetually.

Most of the temples had a dais where sat the chief or priest who presided. This was a modeled clay platform on the floor near the altar. Occasionally, there was also a clay seat built against one wall. Temple floors were prepared before the walls were constructed. At the time the floor was outlined with

REMAINS OF ANCIENT NORRIS BASIN TEMPLE, WITH MOLDS OF WALL POSTS OUTLINING THE FLOOR PATTERN, AND CLAY SEAT AND ALTAR WELL PRESERVED

trenches, puddled clay was spread over the area and baked hard with fire.

Dwelling houses, built in the same manner as temples, were seldom larger than 20 by 25 feet, and usually were smaller. In the center of the floor was a fireplace, a simple basin a few inches deep, surrounded by a thick, elevated clay rim.

Today, the temples and houses are gone—archaeologists find merely the molds of the lower ends of the wall uprights. But occasionally by good fortune, they find parts of charred, collapsed remains of burned buildings preserved. When these sparse remains are carefully uncovered they are sufficient to demonstrate that the buildings were similar to those seen centuries later by white men. The early explorers described the temples as having carved and painted wooden pillars, and walls hung with colorfully patterned mats. And they were particularly impressed by sculptured wooden figures—human, eagles, serpents, and other symbolic forms—that graced the fronts and roofs of temples and served as tribal emblems.

The elaborateness of the temple mound culture, as well as the large populations represented by numerous towns, depended upon intensive agriculture. Corn was the most important plant, and its planting, ripening and harvesting played a major role in ceremonial life. Beans, second in food value to corn, were grown in various shapes and colors. Like corn, they could be stored almost indefinitely to provide security against the uncertainties of wild food resources. While corn contains mainly starches and sugars that supply energy, beans are rich in protein and are a substitute for meat. These two cultivated plants, supplemented by pumpkins and squashes, were the bulwark of the large populations, but wild plants were important too. Among these were native sweet potatoes, marsh potatoes, several varieties of smilax roots, and various nuts, berries and fruits. Fishing and hunting were the only sources of meat, for there were no domestic animals except dogs.

In spite of their advanced culture, the temple mound Indians were still a Stone Age people because they lacked knowledge of metallurgy—the process of smelting ores to extract metals. Their household and hunting equipment, made from the same materials that were used by the Woodland Indians, included similar tools for similar tasks. Nor was their chief weapon, the bow and arrow, any more effective.

However, temple mound pottery was distinctive, the result of greater technical skill and more variation in esthetic ideas. The shapes of the vessels also had more variety—shallow bowls, large basins, long-necked bottles and jars with handles. Smooth and often highly polished surfaces were characteristic of this pottery whose main types of decoration were painting and modeling. The painting consisted of designs in red ochre on the natural buff

POTTERY DECORATED WITH RED PAINT

background, with the free-hand designs skillfully adapted to the vessel shapes. Modeled decoration was simpler, conventionalized human and animal heads being the most frequent motifs. One other type of decoration—stamping—deserves mention because it is an example of borrowed ideas. When the temple mound Indians infiltrated the southeastern region, stamped decoration had reached the peak of its development and popularity among the local Woodland tribes. It was not long until the newcomers adopted the technique and began to express their own artistic ideas in the designs they carved on the stamping paddles.

More utilitarian were the large shallow basins called "salt pans," because many fragments are found around salt springs where they had been used for evaporating salt. However, the pans undoubtedly had many other uses, since numerous fragments also are found on town sites. Even small pieces are interesting to archaeologists because their outer surfaces bear the impressions of woven fabrics and are the main source of information on weaving. The fabric impressions were incidental to the process of their construction. Although made by the coiling method, they

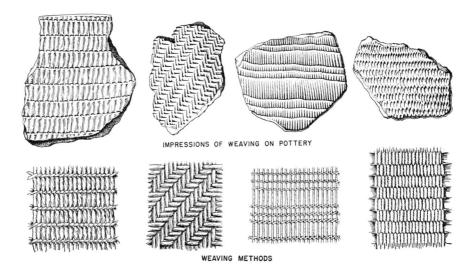

IMPRESSIONS OF WEAVING ON POTTERY

WEAVING METHODS

were supported during the process in a cloth-lined depression in the ground. The impressions of the fabrics vary from a cloth-like modern burlap or coarse muslin to open netting and matting. It may certainly be assumed from this that the people wore clothing made of woven fabrics, but beyond that fact there is no direct evidence of the nature of the garments.

It is the graves of prehistoric peoples that reveal most of the information about their costumes and ornaments. But no graves of the early Hiwassee Island people have yet been discovered in eastern Tennessee. Elsewhere in the South, the dead were sometimes buried in special funeral mounds. Costume and ornament information from those sites corresponds to evidence from a later phase in eastern Tennessee when graves were numerous.

One explanation of why excavations in eastern Tennessee sites failed to locate the burials of the early phase may be found in eyewitness accounts of De Soto's expedition in 1540. These describe special mortuary buildings, located outside the towns proper, where the dead were deposited. Still another explanation coming from early records indicates that some of the tribes cremated the bodies of the dead in the homes where they had lived. Whatever the reason, the whereabouts of the burials of the Hiwassee Island phase remains a mystery.

The age of temple mounds continued into the full light of recorded history, when many of its peoples can be identified with known Indian tribes. Among these were the "people of one fire" whose story follows.

Chapter 6
"People of One Fire"

GIRL'S COSTUME AND ORNAMENTS

"People of One Fire"

Fire to the Muskhogeans was the manifestation on earth of the supreme being whose heavenly symbol was the sun, and when they used the expression "people of one fire," it had a mystical significance. Tribes who together celebrated the annual ceremony of rekindling the sacred fire were henceforth considered spiritually as well as politically allied. In the historic period even white traders sometimes used the phrase "people of one fire" to designate any type of alliance between tribes or peoples.

Political alliances were characteristic of all of the Muskhogean-speaking tribes but reached the highest development among those historically known as the "Creeks." Long before Columbus, they organized a great confederacy that included more than a dozen Muskhogean tribes, and others as well. Although a number of other confederations existed among the peoples who shared the Mississippian culture, this was the largest of such prehistoric, intertribal alliances. And some of its member tribes were the dominant groups in Tennessee's late temple mound period.

The Indians of the confederacy were not called "Creeks" in prehistoric times, for "Creek" is not an Indian name. It originated from "Ocheese Creek" which was the English traders' name for the Ocmulgee River in Georgia where the Ocheese tribe lived at the time. The traders, who at first referred to the tribe as the

"Ocheese Creek Indians," gradually dropped the Ocheese part and merely called them "Creeks." Since this was one of the most important tribes of the confederacy, the name "Creeks" was eventually used for all of the tribes that belonged to that great alliance.

The strength of the confederacy lay in the artful policies of the Creeks in incorporating alien tribes of different cultures. As a result, the Creeks themselves became cosmopolitan in their outlook, and the incorporated tribes often occupied positions of great prestige among them. Culturally, the peoples of the confederacy became the heirs of the early temple mound and Hopewellian traditions, and the ways of life of all of the allied tribes were enriched by the integration of diverse elements.

The social and political framework of the confederacy had three strong supports—the clan, the "talwa," and the "fires." Creek clans, like all clans, were extensions of the ordinary family group to include persons who considered themselves related by descent from a remote or even mythical ancestor. Among most of the southern Indians, relationship was traced on the mother's side—all children belonged to their mother's clan. Aside from the fact that clans regulated marriage (a person could not marry anyone who belonged to his own clan), all members had obligations toward each other. Since nine of the clans existed among all or most of the constituent tribes of the confederacy, a Creek had clan brothers and sisters wherever he went. Thus, kinship ties formed a network of personal relationships that strengthened the political bonds.

The "talwa," which literally translated from the Muskhogean language meant "town," was actually a tribal territorial province that included a capital town which was a ceremonial and political center plus a number of associated villages that surrounded it. The tribe and the province were known by the same name as the capital town. Some of the main talwas held sway over very large areas because of the number of settlements that were attached to them. Each talwa's warriors could be recognized by the special designs that were used for face painting. And each capital town had its own special emblem such as an eagle, serpent, fish, or alligator which was represented by wooden sculptures, carvings on tobacco pipes, and designs on other ceremonial objects. Since the talwa's capital was the center where the great annual ceremonies were held, people from all of the associated villages congregated there at least once a year. This provided a means of fostering close relationships within a tribe.

The "fires" divided the confederacy into two classes of talwas, one group dedicated to maintaining peace and the other to waging wars. Because the Creeks regarded white as the color of peace, happiness and sacredness, and red as the color of war and bloodshed, peace towns were known as white towns, and war towns as red. The members of each of these groups claimed to be "people of one fire" because they celebrated together the annual rekindling of the sacred fire. The white towns were called "the old beloved towns" and were places of refuge where human blood was never shed intentionally. Even criminals and enemies could find temporary refuge in such towns, although they ran the risk of being forced out and killed beyond its limits. Peace treaties were consummated in white towns, while wars were initiated in red towns. When war was decided upon, the head chief sent red war clubs to each sub-chief. If the clubs were colored half red, it signified that only young warriors were to go, but when the clubs were all red, it was a summons for fighting men of all ages. The faces, bodies and weapons of Creek warriors were painted red, and red banners streaked with black—symbols of blood and death—were hung in the towns during war. The leader of the warriors carried a red war pole, and when scalps were taken, they too were painted red.

Red and white towns played against each other in the ball games that were side attractions at ceremonial and social events. All arrangements for this game, called "the brother of war" by the Creeks, were made by the Big Warrior. He was highest ranking war official, a combination chief of police and four-star general. The game, similar to modern lacrosse, was so rough that players often had broken arms and legs, and occasionally were killed. According to the traditions of the Creeks, their ancestors fought so hard against the earlier inhabitants of the country that finally there was none left who was willing to oppose them. Yet they still yearned for battle. Since the original tribes of the confederacy had pledged themselves never to fight against each other, they were obliged to find some substitute for warfare. The ball game, being the nearest thing to a battle, filled the requirements and hence was called "the brother of war." While this game was a more or less violent outlet for aggressive and competitive emotions, it was also a factor in establishing friendly relationships.

The red and white fires, with their contrasting but balanced peace and war functions, accomplished more than the uniting of the talwas; they were basic factors in the political operation and growth of the confederacy. For example, when alien tribes were incorporated, they usually joined the white fire. Thus, the talwas furnished the ceremonial and administrative units, the clans provided the personal bonds between individuals, and the fires cemented both into the strong political fabric of the great confederation.

Within its framework most of the southern Indian cultures of the temple mound age attained their final developments, and the whole southeastern region became connected by a vast network of trails and water routes. Products and ideas from many towns and tribes flowed in all directions along these routes to further unify the cultures of the peoples.

The populations of the eastern and middle areas of Tennessee were deeply involved in the fortunes of the Creek confederacy. In eastern Tennessee large centers like Hiwassee Island became member talwas of the confederacy, and undoubtedly the same was true of some in Middle Tennessee.

The late phase of the temple mound age in eastern Tennessee, the Dallas culture, received its name from the large site that occupied both sides of the river at Dallas Island. Although this Dallas culture retained the basic pattern of the earlier Hiwassee Island phase, it differed in many details.

A significant difference lay in the burial customs. Graves were scattered throughout Dallas towns, close to the homes where the deceased had lived. This contrasted with the custom in the earlier phase of excluding the dead from the community of the living. The Dallas graves have furnished an intimate picture of costumes, ornaments, tools, containers and weapons. Apparently, little was left for the relatives to inherit when a Dallas Indian

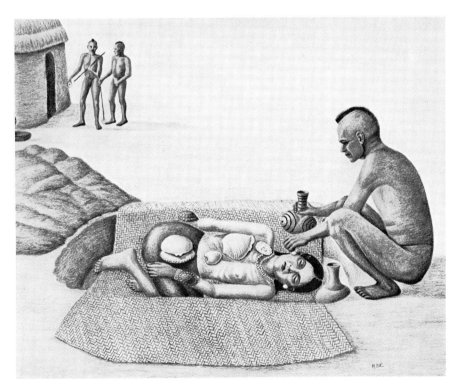

BURIAL OF A DALLAS GIRL

died, for most of the personal property was placed in the grave.
Historical accounts explain that the Creeks thought the souls of
the dead faced long journeys, beset with many hazards, before

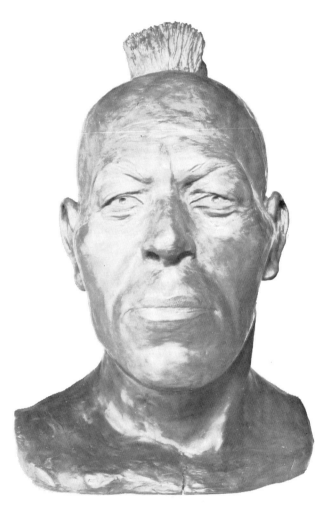

FACIAL FEATURES RECONSTRUCTED OVER THE SKULL OF
A DALLAS MAN

reaching the happy hunting ground. Hence, they equipped the dead with everything necessary for the spirit's safe passage to the other world. Dallas graves appear to reflect such beliefs and customs.

The skeletons reveal how short the average life span was—very few persons surviving to the age of forty-five. The large number of children's skeletons indicates that the first few years of life particularly were fraught with hazards. The young mother who died in childbirth was buried with her stillborn infant. And the warrior, if he survived battles with enemies, succumbed from disease during middle age, tortured as well by arthritis and abscessed teeth.

Only the strongest survived the natural perils of existence and some of the rigorous Creek customs. For example, each morning men, women, children—not excluding babies—were obliged to bathe in the river as soon as they awakened. Custom demanded that they submerge four times, even in the cold of winter, unless snow was on the ground, when it was then permissible to roll four times in the snow instead. This was supposed to make them strong of body and free from sin.

The men were of medium height and muscular, with broad foreheads and often aquiline noses. Their faces were long, their jaws square and their cheek bones prominent. The women were delicately built, with small hands and feet. Their faces were oval-shaped and their features pleasing.

The Dallas people had high standards of craftsmanship, and their products—whether of stone, shell, metal, or pottery—show a combination of skill, imagination and artistic ability. This is evident in their pottery which has a variety of shapes and decorations. They made the same large basins, impressed with textiles, that were used during the earlier Hiwassee Island phase. However, the handles of their jars were different. The earlier handle type was a thick loop of clay, the lower end of which was riveted through the wall of the vessel, and the upper end molded to the rim. The typical Dallas handle was a flat strap of clay molded at both ends. Other pottery products included ladles, colanders, bottles, bowls in all imaginable shapes, ornaments, pipes, and even a few tools. Most of the pottery vessels had some sort of decoration, if only notching around the rim. A number had designs incised into the clay while it was still soft, others were ornamented with modeled figures, and sometimes whole vessels were made in the shape of animals or humans.

Painted pottery was rare and was apparently obtained in trade from Middle Tennessee. It differed from the red-painted pottery of earlier times, not only in color but also in technique. The technique is called negative painting because the unpainted portions form the design. This is done by covering the pattern of the design with wax, and then painting the rest of the surface. When the vessel is fired, the wax disappears, and the light design stands out against a dark background. Negative painting has been found

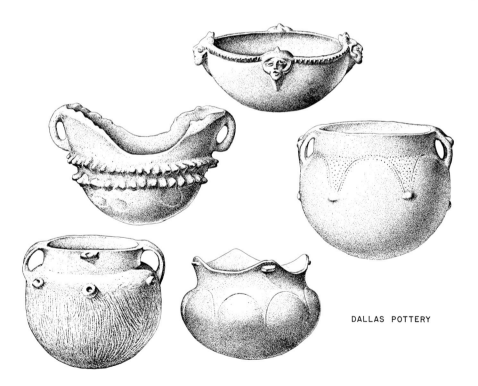

DALLAS POTTERY

in only a few places in the United States, and one of these centers is in the Cumberland Valley near Nashville. Vessels, probably made in the Cumberland area, occur in Alabama, Georgia and in the Dallas culture sites of eastern Tennessee. Negative painting was one of the ancient arts of the Mexican and South American civilizations, but no clues exist to explain how the late temple mound Indians learned the technique. Few suitable waxes were available to them, except possibly from the bayberry shrub or from bumblebee nests, since there were no honeybees in North America in prehistoric times. The wide distribution of this beautiful pottery is an example of how the products that were specialties of one group circulated throughout the confederacy, and

NEGATIVE PAINTED POTTERY

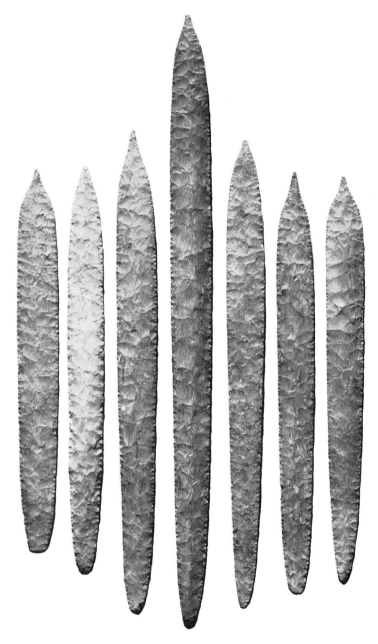

FLINT BLADES MADE BY DUCK RIVER INDIANS (CENTRAL BLADE IS
NEARLY TWENTY-EIGHT INCHES LONG)

even beyond its territory.

A second instance of this was the flint chipping specialization of another Middle Tennessee group who lived along the Duck River near its confluence with the Tennessee. Some of the most extraordinary flint work ever made by man came from the hands of the Duck River Indians. The greatest of their masterpieces were buried long ago beneath the grave of a dead warrior. These included forty-six symbolic flint objects, exquisitely chipped to represent eagle claws, turtles, sun disks, axes, maces and swords. Among the eleven sword-like blades, one is nearly twenty-eight inches long and none is less than seventeen inches. Two sculptured stone images, one portraying a man and the other a woman, were buried beneath the flint pieces. Perhaps the grave was that of some honored chieftain, the guardian in death as well as in life of the treasures of the tribe.

The Duck River Indians did not keep all of their handiwork at home, for it was in great demand by surrounding tribes. The long swords and other ceremonial flints circulated just as widely as the negative painted pottery. Many pieces have been found in the great ceremonial centers throughout the South, including the Dallas site in eastern Tennessee. The Duck River Indians were located about thirty miles south of two large flint quarries, one of which provided the enormous boulders necessary to make the large sword blades. Even today, partly undermined boulders can be seen, just as they were left by the Indians during their last quarrying work. Incredible skill was required to break up the large boulders and secure slabs thin enough to be worked into the long swords. The flint from these quarries can be easily recognized by its peculiar grain and color, and the finished objects always exhibit similarities in workmanship. Regardless of where such pieces are found they can be identified as having been made by the Duck River Indians. Whether these Middle Tennessee peoples were incorporated in the confederacy or merely maintained trade relationships cannot be determined. At least their culture definitely belonged to the temple mound tradition.

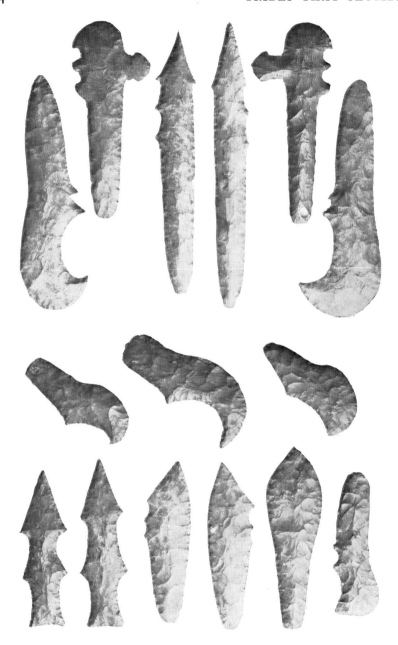

FLINT CEREMONIAL OBJECTS MADE BY DUCK RIVER INDIANS (MACE-
LIKE FORMS, SYMBOLIC EAGLE CLAWS AND AXES)

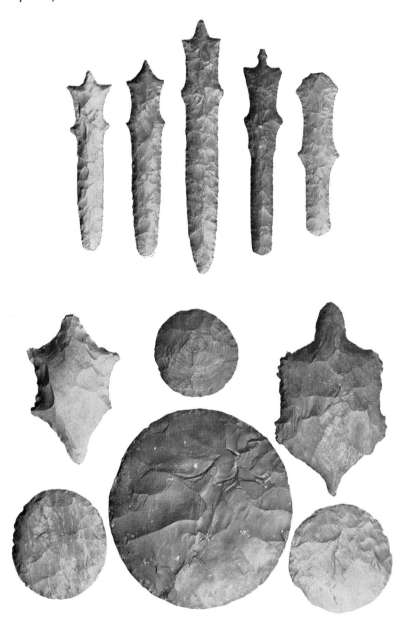

FLINT CEREMONIAL OBJECTS MADE BY DUCK RIVER INDIANS (MACE-LIKE
FORMS, SYMBOLIC TURTLES AND SUN DISKS)

One of the rarest objects of this period is the ceremonial monolithic axe, so called because its blade and handle were carved
from a single block of stone. Very few have been found, and
only rarely more than one at a single site, which suggests that
they were ritual objects. An example from the Dallas site ex-
hibits the same form and flawless finish of the dozen or so others
found in the southern United States. Ceremonial axes with copper blades and wooden handles were also made, the shape cor-
responding to that of the monolithic axes. Three such copper

SCULPTURED STONE IMAGES APPROXIMATELY EIGHTEEN INCHES HIGH FROM WILSON
COUNTY, TENNESSEE

blades, the largest being fifteen inches long and six inches wide at the bit, were found on a Dallas culture site near Kingston, Tennessee. They had been carefully wrapped in cane matting and placed with other beautiful objects in the grave of a chieftain.

Copper was worked in the same manner as it had been thousands of years earlier by the Archaic Indians. The nuggets of pure metal were beaten into thin sheets and, in the case of thick objects like axe blades, several layers of the sheets were hammered together until they formed a solid mass. The final shaping and finishing was done by grinding with an abrading stone. More

MONOLITHIC AXE FOUND IN A DALLAS INDIAN'S GRAVE

elaborate than the axes were the ornaments cut from the thin sheets and decorated with embossed designs. The embossing process consisted of carving the design on a wooden die and then pressing the metal over the die until the design appeared in relief. Headdresses, breastplates and large plaques were decorated in this manner. Ear ornaments were carved wooden disks plated with copper. All of the elaborate copper objects appear to have been worn only by people of prominence. Throughout the South, from Florida to Oklahoma, such articles and their decorative designs vary only slightly. At least some of the copper has been identified as coming from the Ducktown deposits in eastern Tennessee.

The carving and engraving of shell was another art in which

CEREMONIAL COPPER AXE BLADES FROM ROANE COUNTY, TENNESSEE

the late temple mound builders excelled. Among the Dallas Indians, disk-shaped gorgets were the most outstanding examples
of this art. Cut from the walls of large marine conchs, the disks
range in diameter from an inch and a half to seven inches. Two
small holes, drilled close together near the edge, indicate that
they were worn suspended from necklaces, with the concave surfaces showing elaborately engraved designs.

The cross design, which was used frequently, represented either the four quarters of the world or the sun, since it was occasionally surrounded by a sun circle motif. However, its four

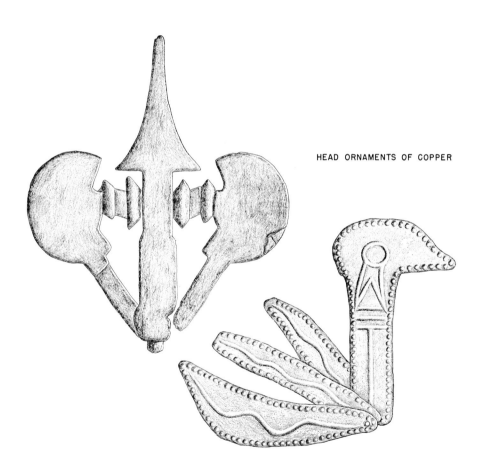

HEAD ORNAMENTS OF COPPER

equal arms may have symbolized the Creek confederacy itself which was founded by four legendary towns. The cross in Mexico was a symbol of both rain and fertility. Whatever meaning it may have had for the temple mound Indians, it was surely an important one, for it was used on ceremonial pottery vessels and other objects, as well as on the shell gorgets.

Another design with a central symbol composed of three radiating whorls surrounded by a pattern of concentric circles had the scalloped edge that completed the design. Variations of the central symbol, called a triskelion, are also found in the Old World where they appear on many different objects.

Animal motifs also were present on the gorgets. An intricately balanced design was formed by a coiled rattlesnake with gaping jaws. Pileated woodpeckers, wild turkeys and spiders were depicted with a combination of realism and stylized art. All of these creatures—snakes, birds and insects—figured in the mythology of the Muskhogean Indians.

Human figures, too, were portrayed in the gorget designs. Dancers, dressed in feathered costumes to represent eagles, and brandishing swords like those made by the Duck River Indians, were fitted harmoniously into the circular space. The eagle, held sacred by the Muskhogeans, was often represented in their art.

A bird face, highly conventionalized, was adapted to a mask-like gorget. Two holes formed the eyes which were surrounded by engraved designs that resemble the markings around the eyes of falcons. The eagle in Muskhogean art was often depicted with these same markings. On the masks, wavy lines issuing from the eyes have been thought to represent tears, hence the motif has been called the "weeping eye." This may have special significance because the masks, found lying on the chests or faces of burials, show no evidence of having been worn in life. The two eye holes, which were the only means of suspension, never show any wear from a cord. Apparently, the masks were part of the death ritual, with the weeping eye symbolizing sorrow.

Lavish use of shell beads characterized the Dallas Indians' costumes—as many as ten thousand have been found with a single skeleton. Small fresh water and marine shells, unaltered except for perforations, formed necklaces or were sewn onto garments and headbands. Beads cut from the cores of marine conchs were

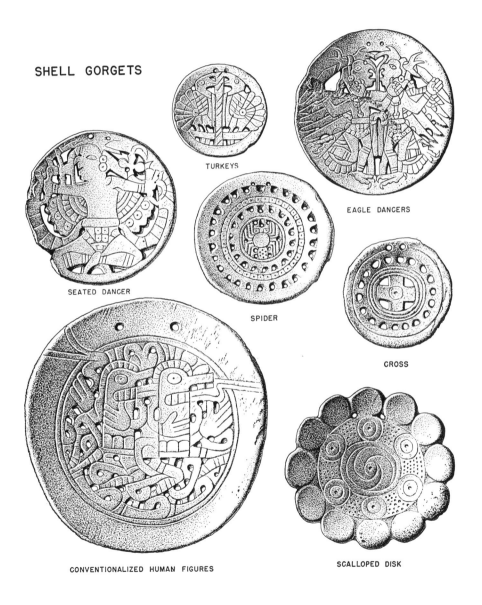

SHELL GORGETS

TURKEYS

EAGLE DANCERS

SEATED DANCER

SPIDER

CROSS

CONVENTIONALIZED HUMAN FIGURES

SCALLOPED DISK

used in the same manner and also for legbands, belts and wrist cuffs. While most of these beads were small, having disk, globular or tubular shapes, others were as large as walnuts. Conch shell cores were also carved into pin-shaped ornaments with bulbous or mushroom-shaped heads. These pins appear to have been inserted through the ear lobes, although they may occasionally have been worn in the hair.

Fresh water pearls, skillfully perforated with very small drills, were another source of beads. One necklace contained a thousand pearls, and individual examples a half inch in diameter have been found in Dallas sites of eastern Tennessee. The fabulous size and beauty of the pearls worn by the Indians impressed the early

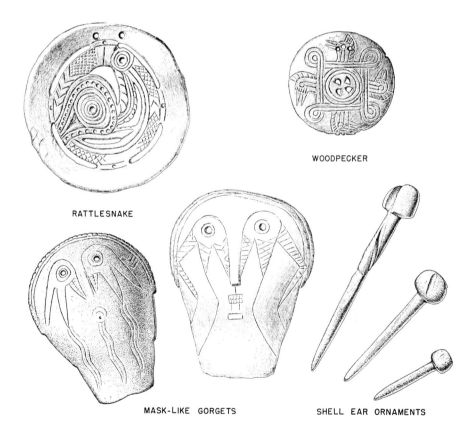

WOODPECKER

RATTLESNAKE

MASK-LIKE GORGETS

SHELL EAR ORNAMENTS

Spanish and English explorers who, seeing in them a possible source of wealth, secured as many as they could by barter.

Despite their elaborate handicrafts, the Dallas Indians lived in simple homes. Large posts, spaced widely apart, formed the supporting framework for the walls which were covered with cane and clay plaster, and the roof was either thatched with grass or covered with slabs of bark. Inside, beds which were simple platforms covered with cane mats were built around the walls. An early traveler once said that the Indians told him they raised the beds above the ground in order to make it harder for the fleas to reach the occupants in a single hop. The fireplace in the center of the floor was a clay-lined basin about a foot in diameter and had a raised rim like those in the Hiwassee Island houses. Pottery and other odds and ends were stored under the beds, but food and various kinds of equipment not in immediate use were packed away in the rafters, out of the reach of children, dogs, and rodents. These were primarily winter houses; during the summer, cooking, eating and other activities were carried on outside under open arbors.

Historic descriptions of the customs of the Creeks provide a picture of prehistoric life in the towns of the late temple mound period, including the Dallas towns of eastern Tennessee. Life centered about the public square which was an outdoor council ground, oblong in shape and encompassing about half an acre. The square was flanked on all four sides by buildings which had only three walls, the fourth side being open to the square. Each building was divided into three stalls by partitions about four feet high. Within the stalls were two or three tiers of mat-covered benches, each rising a foot or so above the one in front. It was customary to add a new mat each year, leaving the old one underneath, so that after some years the seats became well upholstered.

The public square was laid out according to the four cardinal directions. The west building was reserved for the chief and for members of his clan who performed minor functions. The south one was occupied by a group of officials who acted as lieutenants

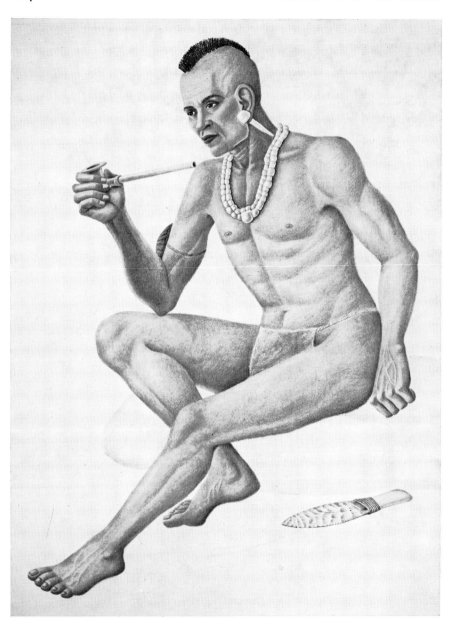

DALLAS MAN

of the chiefs and had charge of certain rites during ceremonies. The seats of the warriors were in the north building. Warriors were divided into three classes: the highest war officials, the main warriors who were assistants and messengers for the officials, and the minor warriors who had not yet achieved distinction in battle. The east building was reserved for "boys," youths who still had not been to war, and for visitors.

The public square was the basis of local government. There the men spent much of their time, each day assembling in council to hear complaints and decide squabbles, receive visitors, and discuss town affairs. The principal chief, called the "miko," was the head of civil life and the governor of the town. He directed the decisions of the council and conducted negotiations with outsiders. He also had charge of the town's food supplies and set the dates for important ceremonies. As elected head of the council and spokesman for the tribe, eloquence was one of his main qualifications. Speech making among the Creeks was a high art and greatly admired, and no miko could be successful without having oratorical gifts. This ability often served him well in talking himself out of embarrassing situations, for both the prosperity and misfortunes of the town were attributed to him. A second chief, called the "twin miko," was, most of the time, a sort of vice-president in charge of the public square. However, when a head chief became old and feeble, the twin chief took over more duties, the elder then becoming chief emeritus and remaining highly respected for the rest of his days.

The real rulers of a town and, perhaps, of the confederacy as well, were a group of revered elders, referred to as the "beloved men." Although too old for active service as warriors and officials, they had garnered during their lifetime the experience which made them the chief's main counselors. The chief relied upon the judgment of these elder statesmen in matters of war and diplomacy, and especially in regard to ceremonial practices. Early each morning the men congregated in the public square to purify themselves with what they called the "asi" or "white drink," and

DALLAS CHILDREN

the early white traders called the "black drink." This was a very strong tea, dark brown in color with white froth on top, made from the shrub *Ilex vomitoria*. Its principal, and almost immediate effect, was to cause vomiting. The Creeks believed that the drinking of this tea purified them from sin and made them invincible in war. Moreover, they considered it the proper way to cement friendship. Hence, the white traders soon learned that it was profitable to observe the custom, although it is doubtful that they ever acquired any real taste for the tea! The ritual of the black drink was governed by a rigid set of customs. The drink itself, prepared by the chief's lieutenants under his direction, was brewed over a fire in the center of the square. Persons of the highest rank were served first, and so on down the line until all had partaken. Usually the drink made three or four rounds, time out being allowed between each round for getting rid of the previous dose outside the square.

This ritual was strictly for men. If women or children ventured into the square during the ceremony, they were scratched, either with snake teeth fastened in wood or with a garfish jaw. Scratching was a customary punishment for children—to let out the evil that made them do wrong. In this way the children were also taught to endure pain and the sight of blood, something they would frequently experience in later life.

The solemnity of the daily town council meeting was surpassed only by the great assemblies of the confederacy. These took place in some important town once each year. Only the most celebrated chiefs and warriors were allowed to speak at such national meetings. The conduct of Creek government, both local and federal, was not as democratic as might be supposed, because all real business was conducted and final decisions made by the chiefs. The assembly of the confederacy merely sat in session to hear what was done. The years of experience that the chiefs acquired in handling the problems of the confederacy was evident in the shrewd statesmanship they displayed in dealing with the white men in historic times.

During winter the town council was held indoors in a large
building that the Creeks called the "house with a big room."
The white traders, however, called it the "hot house," because of
its stifling heat and smokiness. Some of these described by the
early traders were circular in shape with huge pillars that supported a high conical roof. Members of the council sat on tiers of
benches that encircled the wall, the central area being reserved
for the special ceremonies and the speakers who addressed the
council. Structures of this rotunda type were built upon the fifth
level of the temple mound on Hiwassee Island, although later
buildings were rectangular.

At the Dallas site, council buildings were square in shape;
around the walls a raised bench of clay, five feet wide and cov-

DALLAS ROTUNDA TYPE TEMPLE ON FIFTH LEVEL OF HIWASSEE ISLAND MOUND

ered with mats, provided seats for the council members. The
bench was divided by partitions into four sections which apparently corresponded to the four divisions of the outdoor square.
A square altar of clay for the sacred fire occupied the center of
the floor. One building had a small annex adjacent to the south
wall, and connected to the main structure by a narrow passage;
it evidently was the repository for ritual objects.

When important Creek council meetings were convened, a special fire was laid in a spiral pattern on the floor. Short lengths of
cane were placed obliquely across each other, beginning at the
center, the coil proceeding counter-clockwise until a spiral ten
or twelve feet in diameter had been formed. Then the outer end
was lighted, and the fire crept slowly around the spiral. When
the flames reached the center, it was the signal for the council

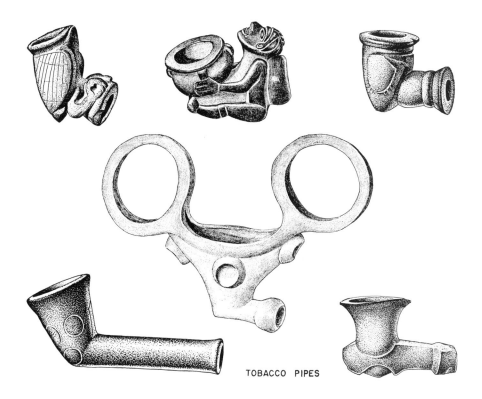

TOBACCO PIPES

meeting to adjourn. Thus, the fire not only furnished light and
heat, but also acted as a ceremonial timepiece.

During councils, the "black drink" ritual followed the lighting
of the fire, after which a ceremonial pipe was passed from person
to person. The pipe and a special tobacco pouch, as well as other
ritual objects, were kept in a sanctuary. The pouch was made
from the skin of some particular animal, bird, or snake that was
the emblem of the chief's clan. Before the smoking began, the
pipe, its long stem decorated with eagle feathers, was laid at
the chief's feet. He smoked first, blowing puffs ceremoniously
toward the Great Spirit above the earth, then toward the four
directions, and finally toward his lieutenants. Next, the highest
ranking among these men smoked, and after him, the "great warrior." Thus, the pipe was gradually passed down through the
ranks until all had participated.

When the business on hand was peaceful, a fan-shaped emblem
made of white eagle feathers was displayed. When war was con-
templated, the feathers were tipped with red. The white tail
feathers of the bald eagle, our own national emblem, were held
particularly sacred by the Creeks. A distinguished Creek states-
man named Tomochichi, who was received by King George II
of England in 1734, presented a sheaf of these feathers to the
king, telling him that they were a sign of everlasting peace between the Creeks and the English.

In addition to the public square with its open front buildings,
and the winter council chamber which stood near the square,
each town had a chunkey yard. The latter, a large square court
scraped smooth and level, was used for the game called
"chunkey." This was played with a large disk made from quartzite, granite, or other fine-grained stone. The disks, five to six
inches in diameter and about two inches thick, had concave faces.
Almost perfectly symmetrical and highly polished, they required
a prodigious amount of labor to make. The game was played by
two persons at a time, each carrying a pole eight to ten feet long.
As one of the players rolled the disk down the center of the court,

he and his opponent ran after it, attempting to throw their poles close to the spot where they estimated the disk would stop rolling. The nearest pole gained the player one point, or if actually touching, two points. The game, once described as "running hard labor," provided an outlet for the Creek passion for gambling, with players and spectators alike staking their possessions on the outcome.

Historical records, beginning with those of the De Soto expedition which passed through the territory of the Creek confederacy during the year of 1540, furnish glimpses of the extent and influence of the confederacy. From the founding of Charleston, South Carolina, in 1670 by the English, the Creeks held the balance of power in the rivalry between Spain, France and England for control of the South. However, wilderness politics, dominated by the extraordinary influence of the Creeks throughout the colonial period, could not save the Indians from eventual

STONE DISKS USED IN CHUNKEY GAME

EARLY HISTORIC CREEK COSTUME

disaster. The Creeks were the probable authors of a great inter-tribal conspiracy in 1715–16, called the Yamasee War, which was a revolt against the abuses of the English trading system. Defeat of the Creeks and their allies was largely the result of the age-old enmity between the confederacy and the Cherokee. When the Cherokee were finally induced to side with the colonists, the power of the Creeks was broken. Outlying towns were abandoned, and many groups migrated southward to Florida to become the nucleus of the Seminole nation. Those who remained were gradually won back as allies by the colonies of South Carolina and Georgia whose foothold on the eastern seaboard was threatened by the Spanish in Florida and the French in the Mississippi Valley. In 1813–14 the only serious revolt of the Creeks against the new republic of the United States resulted in their defeat at the hands of Andrew Jackson at the battle of Horseshoe Bend where nearly a thousand warriors were killed. The tribal lands were gradually confiscated between 1814 and 1836, and the last of the remaining Creeks were removed to Indian Territory by 1840.

The "people of one fire," whose grand alliance dominated the Southeast for hundreds of years, owed much of their unity to the bonds which were reinforced each year at their great annual ceremony, the "Busk." This ceremony survived among the exiled Creeks, even until the twentieth century when it was still observed in less elaborate form but with much of its ancient solemnity.

Chapter 7

The Great Busk

DANCERS IMPERSONATING EAGLES

RECONSTRUCTION OF COPPER PLATE FROM THE ETOWAH MOUND IN GEORGIA

The Great Busk

When the sun had reached its zenith in midsummer, the great new year ceremony of the Creeks took place. It was called *Boskita,* which the white traders shortened to "Busk." The ceremony lasted for eight days and was dedicated to rites and ceremonies of a mystical and profoundly religious nature.

The supreme god of the Creeks was known as "Master of Breath," or "The One Above Us." He was believed to reside in the sky and to be the source of warmth, light and life itself. The sun was his symbol in the sky, and fire was his manifestation on earth. Each year the presence of the Master of Breath was renewed by the rekindling of the sacred fire and the other rites of the Busk.

All tribes of the confederacy observed the ceremony, with the groups of white talwas celebrating separately from groups of red talwas. Descriptions of the Busk have come down to us from eighteenth-century white men whom the Creeks had learned to respect and trust.

Through their eyes can be vizualized the great ceremony at one of the typical main towns. It is the time of the new moon in late June or early July. The chief and his assistants have sent out a messenger through the town in order to call all of the men to meet and plan for the coming event. It has been necessary to wait until the corn plants are nearly mature, because the first fruits of the new harvest are to be used in the ceremony. So, the planning committee meets about three weeks in advance when the ears are starting to fill out. At this first session, orders are given to make new pottery vessels and other equipment.

Two weeks now pass during which three more meetings are held to arrange for medicinal herbs, firewood and food. Then they hold a final meeting and set the date. Invitations are prepared for the towns that traditionally share the same fire. The invitations are bundles of seven small sticks about the size of matches which are called the "broken days." One bundle is tied above the chief's seat in the public square and the others are sent to the chiefs of invited towns. Each day a stick is discarded until only three remain. On this day, all the people living in and near the town assemble around the square. The next day, visitors arrive and are assigned camping places. Now only one stick remains. It is the day of the feast, the last before the Busk is to begin.

The feasting lasts from sunrise to sunset. Everyone eats all he possibly can, for tomorrow no food can be taken by the men. Corn, the most valued of all the foods, cannot be eaten before the Busk. If anyone has secretly eaten it beforehand, he must be purified. The purification is a dose of strong medicine and deep, painful scratching with a garfish jaw.

The day's festivities begin in the morning with a dance by the women. Meanwhile, all of the men have seated themselves in their proper places in the square. Then they wait, usually for several hours, until the women make their appearance. The feminine preparations are elaborate. They wear beautiful costumes and adorn themselves heavily with ornaments. This takes endless time, and if after being notified four times, they still delay, two officials start shouting at them to hurry. It is now nearly noon. A little pot of the Busk medicine, brewed from the red roots of a willow plant, is sent to the women. They anoint their turtle shell rattles and imitation war clubs with it just before the dance begins. Each dance leader wears a number of the turtle shell rattles attached to her arms and legs to accent the rhythm of the dance. Four singers furnish music and shake gourd rattles as they sing. Just before the women enter the square, the chief orders a drummer to beat his drum. At the fourth beat, four men take their places at the corners of the square. They are the "dog-whippers" or guards, armed with long sticks that have sharp garfish teeth on the ends. If any woman should dance too slowly, a dog-whipper will scratch her ankles to make her more lively. He will also keep the dancers from leaving, because no woman is ever permitted to go out of the square, except in the case of illness, unless she is willing to have her ornaments confiscated by a dog-whipper.

Now entering the square one at a time are the dance leaders, the first three taking special positions. The fourth leader is followed by the rest of the women who take their places in a great circle around the fire in the center and begin to dance. After two rounds they go out to rest and then come back for two more hours. This entire dance lasts for three hours in the hot summer sun, after which the women welcome a chance to rest because they will dance again in the evening.

It is now mid-afternoon and the next event is a ball game. Young men are the center of attention for the next few hours. This is the "brother of war" game, and only the most stalwart youths are taking part in it. Sides are chosen, with sixty players on each side. Their bodies brilliantly painted, they are dressed in breech clouts and moccasins; attached to the back of the breech clouts are the tails of swift-footed animals. Each player carries two ball sticks shaped somewhat like small tennis rackets, made of hickory and strung with deerskin thongs. Both teams have medicine men hidden in the woods, making medicine as fast as they can. The small ball is made of deer hair covered with deer skin and sewed with deer sinews.

The field is nearly a quarter of a mile long with a goal at each end formed by two uprights and a crossbar. Now the game is about to begin. All the players rush out and throw down their rackets. These must be counted to make sure that each side has the same number. Then the men divide into five squads, with the opposing players facing each other along the two sides of the field. At the mid-point the ball is tossed up by an old man, and the contest is on. A player catches the ball with his rackets, and either runs with it or throws it. The objective is to hit either the goal posts or crossbar with the ball. After each goal, the ball is put back in play at the center of the field. An especially good player must be wary because his opponents will deliberately try to injure him and put him out of the game. When that happens, the other side must also discard a player, but it is certain not to be one of their best.

On the side lines are the scorekeepers, each having ten small sticks for tallies. Whenever a goal is made, a tally is stuck in the ground by the scorekeeper for that team. After ten goals, the

BALL PLAYERS

sticks are withdrawn one at a time to score the subsequent points. The first side to score twenty points wins. Quantities of valuable objects are wagered on the outcome. Point after point is made and, finally, one team is victorious. Then the winning players run to their goal post and perform an exultant dance while the other team takes to its heels. The losing group is jeered at and especially derided by those who bet on them.

At night everyone joins in an informal dance, both men and women taking part. This is a very hilarious affair, and when it is over, the men remain behind to sleep on the benches in the public square.

In the meantime, the chief has directed the preparation of the sacred medicines for the next day. Four men have been sent to get the four large logs for the New Fire Ceremony at dawn. These must be cut from tree limbs that grow toward the sunrise.

The great day dawns, and before it is light the chief summons young men to clean the square. The old fire is put out and all ashes are removed from the fireplace, after which clean sand is spread over it. The town is dark, for all of the fires in it have been extinguished. All the pots that were used over the old fires have been destroyed. In front of the chief's cabin on the square, clean sand is spread for an altar on which the most sacred objects are to be placed.

Just at daylight, young men bearing these objects advance, two at a time. They hand them to the chief who reverently lays them on the sand altar. The objects are the consecrated copper plates, so holy that they are kept in the sanctuary back of the chief's seat and never brought out except during the Busk. Some are shaped like enormous axe blades, others like disks or squares, the most beautiful ones bearing embossed designs of mythical beings. As the rising sun touches them, they reflect the light like flames from their polished surfaces. As in the sacred fire itself, the presence of the Master of Breath is manifested in the gleaming copper plates. Now the fire-maker approaches. Clothed all in white, his feet are shod with white deerskin moccasins tipped with eagle claws. He wears a tunic and a mantle, both of soft white buckskin. On the crown of his head is a tuft of white egret feathers, and bound around his temples is a snowy band of swan's-down. His breastplate is a shining, white shell disk.

Walking slowly and majestically, he enters the secret place behind the chief's seat and returns with the sacred fire drill. Kneeling on the sand over the old fireplace, he summons the spirit of fire by rapidly twirling the drill. First, smoke begins to rise, and then a flame appears. With small splinters he feeds the tiny fire, and then with the white wing of a swan he fans it to a blaze.

The four logs, cut the night before, have been laid in the form of a cross with each of the arms pointing toward a side of the

SACRED FIRE AND CORN RITUAL

square. The fire-maker and his helper push them toward the fire. One of the elder men brings four ears of corn to the head medicine man or high priest. This dignitary has the highest spiritual qualities; his wisdom and knowledge of secret lore are symbolized by his headdress. It is the stuffed body of an owl, so skillfully fashioned that it appears to be alive. The priest has already received from the chief some white blossoms of the wild tobacco plant. Taking an ear of corn, he faces the rising sun beyond the sacred fire. Then he blows on one of the white blossoms and inserts it in the end of the ear. This first ear he lays across two arms of the log cross so that it points toward the chief's seat. After walking solemnly around the fire, he performs the same rite with the other three ears. Thus he invokes the Master of Breath and consecrates to him the first fruits of the new harvest.

Now the household fires of the town are all rekindled from the new fire, and all of the visiting celebrants will carefully transfer some of it to their own homes when the Busk is over.

The ceremony continues with the preparation of the main Busk medicines in the square. Red roots of the willow are used for one, and button snakeroot for the other. The button snakeroot medicine has many minor ingredients, including wild tobacco flowers, spicewood, cedar, various berries, grapevine, mistletoe, horsemint and a piece of oak. These medicines, brewed in special vessels and served to all in order of their rank, are believed to purify the bodies and souls of the people.

The "black drink" has been prepared while the other medicines are being taken. Since this is drunk only to be vomited up later, it is taken by itself. Several hours are required for this elaborate ritual, during which the drink is served in special cups made from large conch shells. Some of these beautiful vessels are engraved with intricate symbols and are so cherished that they are seldom used except during the Busk.

It is now late afternoon and the ceremony is reaching its climax. Two singers, shaking their rattles, rush toward the official guarding the copper objects. This is the beginning of the "long dance."

One at a time, each copper axe or plate is handed to a distinguished warrior by the chief. These warriors carry feathered
staffs and form the central figures in the dance which moves out
the north entrance of the square and returns through the west
entrance. Warriors and young men dance around the two singers who lead the procession. The circuit in and out of the square
is made four times, with the pace increasing to a furious tempo.
The religious fervor reaches its peak with drums throbbing in
time with the stamp of dancing feet and sharp rhythm of the
rattles. Voices of the singers rise higher and higher, until sound,
color and emotion intoxicate the crowd. Suddenly it is over. A
hush falls upon the square, and slowly the people retire. A great
sense of joy and peace fills their hearts. The Master of Breath has
once more blessed them with his presence, and the sins of the
past year are atoned for. As darkness falls, the square is deserted,

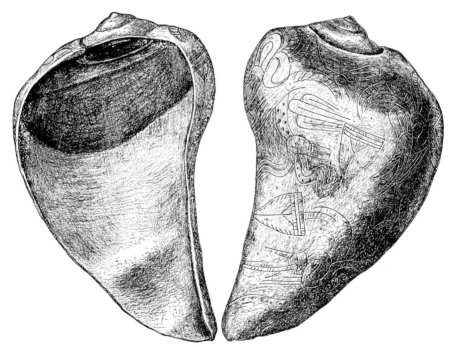

ENGRAVED SHELL VESSEL FOR "BLACK DRINK"

except for the guardian of the sacred fire.

The men who have fasted since sundown of the day before are ready to eat at last. The religious rites of the Busk festival are over, and the next five days will be spent in recreation, with dances held each night. Some of these are danced by men or women only, others by both sexes. Singing accompanies the dances, and each town tries to outdo the others in composing new songs. A friendly rivalry in dancing, singing and ball playing has pervaded the Busk. It has provided a harmless outlet for the competitive emotions while, at the same time, it has strengthened the feeling of friendship and harmony.

On the last day a great orator delivers an address. He admonishes the people to observe all of the ancient customs and rites during the coming year. He tells them that the health and prosperity of all of the people depend on the virtue of each individual, and that sins committed by one person may bring calamity to everyone. He emphasizes this again and again, since one of the purposes of the Busk is to create a mystical bond between those who share the same holy fire. Then he tells everybody to depart for home in peace. Thus ends the great Busk ceremony.

The annual festival helped to unify the tribes of the confederacy, and alien tribes adopted it when they became members. The ideas of peace, law and friendship dominated the whole ceremony. White was its prevailing color, and the day when the new fire was kindled was called the "white day." Only white feathers were used in the square, and the smoke from the sacred fire and tobacco pipes was called the "white smoke." Some symbolic meaning was attached to every act and every object used. Yet, in spite of the main spirit of peace, the symbols of war were ever present. The ancient Creeks realized that they must promote and recognize the warlike virtues, or they would fall prey to their enemies. During the Busk, therefore, warriors were advanced to higher ranks and youths who had won distinction in battle received new war names.

The objects and symbolism of the Busk were known far beyond the country of the Creek confederacy. The member tribes were respected by other Indian nations, for their unity made them strong in war, while the peace in their land made them prosperous. They contracted alliances with distant tribes and cemented these friendships by sharing their sacred fire. Thus, the great southern ceremony and its ritual objects gradually spread over much of eastern North America.

The origin of the Busk is unknown, although in certain features it resembled ceremonies of the Mexican Indians. One of the most ancient gods of Mexico, worshipped by all of the peoples, was the Fire God, also called "Lord of the Year," who was symbolized by a white hummingbird. Each year a festival was held in his honor, and a priest, as the fire-maker at the Busk, kindled a new fire by twirling a wooden drill between his hands. The new fire was then carried to the homes. This was a yearly event and not so elaborate as the New Fire Ceremony observed every fifty-two years. The annual new fire festival of the Aztecs took place at the end of their year, at the time of our January, and not at the ripening of the first corn, as among the Creeks. But another Aztec ceremony occurred in July. It was the festival in honor of the "Goddess of Young Corn" which, like the Creek Busk, lasted for eight days. Not until after the final ritual had been performed were the people permitted to eat corn of the new harvest, a custom likewise observed by the Creeks. Moreover, in both regions, men and women had to remain apart during the ceremonies.

The sacredness of fire and corn formed old and fundamental elements in Indian life. By themselves they are not sufficient to link the southern Indians with the great civilizations of Mexico. Yet the temple mounds and the Busk with its symbolism, as well as the fine arts of the temple mound Indians, have deep roots in the cultures of Middle America.

Chapter 8

"Children of the Sun"

YUCHI TOTEM TALES

"Children of the Sun"

"*Tsoyaha yuchi,*" meaning "We are children of the sun from faraway," was the answer of the South's most mysterious Indians when asked who they were. *Tsoyaha,* "children of the sun," was the name they called themselves. But other Indians, unwilling to accept this claim of divine ancestry, called them merely the *Yuchi,* or "faraway people." The name Yuchi, or Euchee, can still be found on the maps of East Tennessee.

Very few Indian tribes have ever been known by the names which they actually called themselves. Many of those used by the white men were names given by neighboring tribes. The origin of these names can often be traced to peculiar customs or features of a tribe, or the characteristics of the country where the tribe lived. Frequently, a group was designated by a word that meant "people who speak a different language." The name Muskogee, which was applied to one of the dominant tribes of the Creek confederacy, was originally an Algonquian word meaning "swamp." The name Chisca, which was one of the names for the Yuchi, meant "root people" in the Creek language. Thus, a single tribe often had as many different names as it had neighbors.

Yuchi was only one of the many names by which these Indians, who called themselves "Children of the Sun," were known. That is why they are such a mystery. The first time that history takes notice of them was in 1540 when De Soto was told of a rich province called Chisca where copper and gold were mined. De Soto sent out scouts to verify the tale of precious metals, but they returned with discouraging news. They spoke of a trail that led over high mountain ridges and was far too difficult for the expedition to attempt.

The next reference to these people is in connection with a battle that took place in 1566 between Spanish soldiers and some Chisca Indians. The battle was fought in a fortified village where the people lived in "underground" houses. This type of structure is one of the important clues that has helped to identify these people. When archaeologists excavated old Yuchi town sites in eastern Tennessee, they discovered that these Indians lived in houses built partly underground, and that their villages were strongly fortified. Thus, archaeology corroborates history in identifying Chisca as one of the many names for the Yuchi.

Another name that scholars have identified with the Yuchi is Westo. This was a fierce tribe that plagued the young colony of South Carolina for over a decade until about 1682. These same Westo Indians were also known as Rickahokans, a mysterious tribe in the early history of Virginia. They came from somewhere west of the Appalachian Mountains and established themselves near the falls of the James River about 1656. A joint expedition of Virginia colonists and their Indian allies was defeated when an attempt was made to dislodge them. Then, for no apparent reason, the Rickahokans suddenly abandoned their Virginia location, only to turn up farther south as the Westos. At about the same time that the Westos were molesting the South Carolinians, others were harassing the Spaniards, by whom they were called Chiscas. Beyond the Appalachians in eastern Tennessee a large Indian town was visited in 1673 by an exploring party from Virginia. In the account of this visit the people were called Tomahittans. The town was fortified by a heavy stockade, a necessary precaution, to judge by the piratical activities of the tribe. The Virginia explorers saw guns and brass kettles that had been stolen from the Spaniards in St. Augustine. One of the white men who remained with the Tomahittans for a year accompanied them on another expedition to rob the Spanish towns that were located about nine days' travel to the south. However, being a loyal Englishman, he objected when a similar attack was proposed against the English settlement of Port Royal in the colony of South Carolina. Since the most persistent marauders of the Spanish and South Carolina

WHITE MEN'S TRINKETS

colonies at this time were the Chisca and Westos, it follows that
Tomahittan was still another name for the Yuchi.

The Algonkin Indians called the same tribe "Tahogalewi,"
a name which appears in a half dozen or more different versions
on early maps, eventually evolving into Hogologe and Hogohee-
gee. And finally, to add to the confusion, the name Yuchi was
spelled in many ways—Hughchee, Euchee, and even Uge. These
names were applied to the Tennessee River by several early English map makers.

Before the end of the seventeenth century, Carolina and Virginia traders were operating beyond the Appalachian Mountains. They did business with both Yuchi and Cherokee towns in
eastern Tennessee. Since the two tribes were often on bad terms,
the traders led a precarious existence. Much as the Indians desired the white man's trinkets, tools and rum, they resented the
increasing demands for more land. Further indignation was
aroused by the dishonest practices of many traders. To make
matters worse, the English, French and Spanish governments frequently incited the tribes against each other in order to claim
greater territories and to obtain slaves. Captives taken in native
raids were sold to the white men.

One of the Yuchi towns on the Hiwassee River, known as
Chestowee, was tragically involved in a three-way altercation.
Chestowee had incurred the enmity of certain Cherokee, following the murder of a Cherokee by some Yuchis. It had also antag-
onized a local trader by the name of Alexander Long. In an argu-
ment over debts, Long, apparently, had been slightly scalped—
at least the record says he had lost some hair. From then on he
swore to get even. Two Cherokee chiefs were in debt to him, and
he induced them to make up a war party and attack Chestowee,
promising them loot and Yuchi slaves. In 1714 the town was taken
by surprise and overwhelmed by the ferocious attack. Those who
escaped the first volleys of the Cherokee guns ran to the big
council house for protection. But the Cherokee, well armed by
the trader, could not be held off by the defenseless Yuchi. Fear-

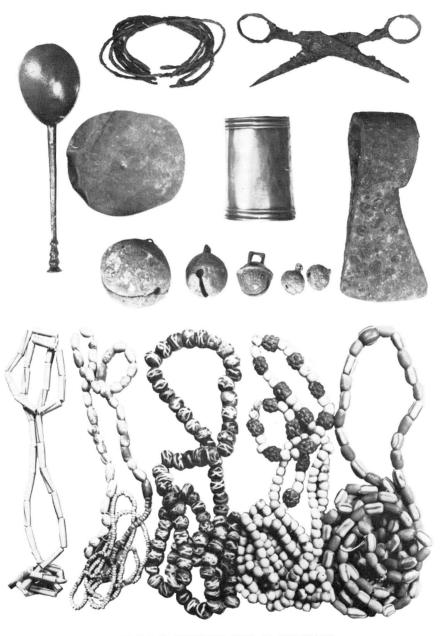

TRADERS' CURRENCY USED IN FUR TRADE

ing enslavement or death by torture, the Yuchi warriors in desperation killed their own families and then committed suicide. When the attackers forced their way into the council house, not a single Yuchi was found alive.

The sudden disaster which befell the town of Chestowee, and the ever-present threat of the Cherokee, caused the rest of the Yuchi to abandon eastern Tennessee. Some settled along the Savannah River, others went to Florida, but most of them moved to the Chattahoochee River in Georgia. They became members of the great Creek confederacy, but did not mix socially with the Creeks any more than was necessary. They remained generally aloof from most other tribes to whom they considered themselves superior. Even the Creeks feared and envied the Yuchi, although they did value them as allies.

These self-styled Children of the Sun played a strange role in the story of Tennessee Indians. They were proud, fearless and aggressive. According to their own traditions they inhabited the southeastern region before the Creeks and other Muskhogean peoples invaded it. Their language has no close relationship with any other American Indian tongue, although it may be distantly related to both Siouan and Muskhogean. The only place where their old towns have been located with certainty is in eastern Tennessee, and there only in a restricted area. Even those towns do not appear to have had a very long existence. They were probably first settled about 1400 A.D., or perhaps even later. There is a strong suspicion that some of the Creeks with an ulterior motive may have encouraged the occupation of this territory by the Yuchi. Nearby in the mountain valleys lived the Cherokee, traditional enemies of the Creeks. Both tribes laid claim to much of the Southeast, and their normal relationship was hostile. Fighting often took place between small war parties, and sudden raids were made upon towns. It was thus that young men earned their war titles and older warriors attained greater distinction. By using the Yuchi province as a buffer state, the Creeks could better protect their own towns.

A very large Yuchi town existed on Ledford Island in the Hiwassee River about twelve miles above its confluence with the Tennessee. A heavy stockade surrounded the town which had a public square and a large ceremonial building. Several miles upstream were two more large towns, one on each side of the river near the mouths of creeks. These streams are called North Mouse Creek and South Mouse Creek. The town on South Mouse Creek was probably Chestowee where the massacre took place. The town nearest to the Cherokee country was close to the confluence of the Ocoee and Hiwassee rivers. It was within a few hundred yards of the Great Indian Warpath, the most important thoroughfare between the northern and southern tribes. The trail, which began in the country of the Creek confederacy and led northward, had branches leading to the Ohio Valley and as far as New England. The Yuchi town on the Ocoee River was well situated to intercept and spy upon any war or trading parties that used the trail. This town was abandoned earlier than those lower down on the Hiwassee River, and later on in the historic period, a group of Cherokee settled there. The locations of two other Yuchi settlements have been discovered. They were on the Tennessee River, one in Roane County and the other in Rhea County. The Rhea County town was the last to be abandoned, probably shortly after the destruction of Chestowee in 1714. Euchee Ferry Road passes by it, and the name persists today, both for the ferry and a small village across the river, which until recent times was known as Euchee Old Fields.

The Yuchi, as already mentioned, built an unusual type of house which was partly underground. First, they dug a pit about two feet deep and from twenty to thirty feet square. Then, they built the walls just inside the edge of the pit. Large upright logs, spaced about two feet apart, formed the framework which was covered with cane lathes and clay plaster, the same as Dallas houses. Against the outside of the walls, the dirt that had been excavated from the pit was heaped up to form an embankment that prevented rain water from seeping onto the floor. This type of construction made a weatherproof home which was also by Indian standards rather spacious for a family that might number anywhere from three to a dozen members. In addition to the sunken floors, Yuchi houses had entrances that differed from those of other southeastern Indians. These entrances were covered vestibules that extended out for several feet and helped to deflect drafts and rain.

It is not surprising that when the Spaniards first saw these houses they had the impression they were built entirely below ground. In spite of the floor pits being only two feet deep, the sloping embankments against the walls made the houses appear even lower than they were, especially when seen from a distance.

A typical Yuchi town had a public square and a council chamber called the "big house." Surrounding this community center, each family had its own private house and lot. Since no family could change its home site without encroaching upon its neighbors, it retained possession of a location for generations, rebuilding the dwelling when necessary over the same old pit. The entire town was usually surrounded by a stockade for protection against enemies. And the inhabitants of particularly vulnerable towns further insured their security by digging deep ditches just beyond the stockades.

The Yuchi were notorious for their strong sense of property rights. Members of the Creek confederacy were cautious about offending them, even to the extent of recognizing their exclusive rights to hunting territories. Indians in general had a definite conception of private property. Among many tribes, individuals had their own personal symbol or brand with which their possessions were marked, and ownership of songs, rituals, medicines, and special occupations was jealously maintained. Indians were also acutely conscious of debts and credits, asserting their rights with firmness and paying their obligations punctually—as the early traders soon discovered. This, perhaps, had much to do with the monopolizing of the Indian trade by close-bargaining Scotchmen who were a match for the Indian bargainers.

Yuchi arts and crafts differed only slightly from those of their neighbors, the Creeks. The women made the same kind of pottery vessels and decorated them similarly by incising and modeling. They excelled in modeling animal and bird heads, often with a touch of humor apparent in the pose or expression of the figures. Since they lived close to nature, their world was one in which animals figured as prominently as people. Myths and tales about various species, handed down from generation to generation, formed a large part of the unwritten literature of the Yuchi, as well as of all American Indians. Many of the stories were humor-

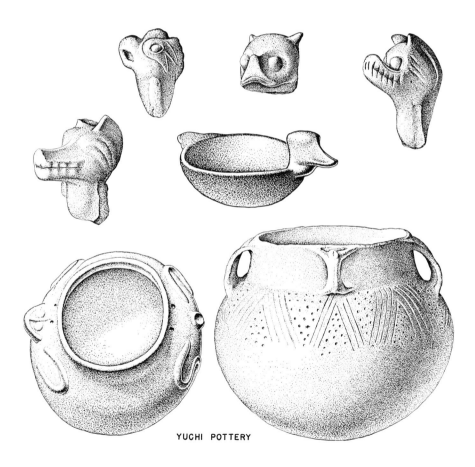

YUCHI POTTERY

ous and were told over and over, purely for entertainment. Others were serious and dramatized the exploits of the totem animals for which the clans were named. The Yuchi, like most of the south-eastern Indians, had clans whose membership was inherited on the mother's side. These clans, with names such as bear, deer, raccoon, fish, turtle, snake, turkey, eagle, etc., had special rela-tionships with the living animals. For example, the Rabbit people could not hunt rabbits, nor could the Turkey people kill turkeys. Yet, if hunters from some other clan did the actual killing, the members could eat the meat or use the feathers and skins. The clan members claimed that they were descended in a mystical way from the animals, which made them relatives of the living species. When animals are regarded in this way they are called totems. The Yuchi Indians particularly enjoyed stories that de-scribed the cunning or wisdom of their own totem. Since clan animals were often used as symbols by the members, it is quite possible that the women sometimes modeled the heads of their own totems on their pottery.

Yuchi men, who never made pots, did model small crude ani-mals out of clay while they sat around telling stories. Perhaps the story teller dramatized his tale with the figurines and later gave them to children for playthings. From an artistic point of view they were hardly worth preserving, but sometimes they were fired with the regular pottery. Strangely enough, these almost shapeless toys have proved to be clues in the Yuchi mystery. As late as 1908 they were still being made by the men of the tribe out in Oklahoma. Besides occurring in the old town sites along the Hiwassee River, they have also been found in Middle Ten-nessee where the Yuchi may have lived before moving into the eastern part of the State.

Archaeology has provided other evidence that the tribe's ear-lier location was in Middle Tennessee—the way the dead were buried. The Yuchi were one of the few Tennessee tribes that laid out the corpse flat on the back with the arms straight at the sides and the legs stretched to the fullest extent. This contrasted markedly with the usual Creek custom which was to place the body on its side in a position that suggested peaceful sleep.

Because of this extended position, when the Yuchi dug a grave, it was a long, narrow oblong with the corners well-squared. The bottom and sides of the grave were lined with slabs of bark, and the cover was made of poles and bark. In this box-like coffin the corpse was protected from any contact with the earth. Occasionally, two bodies were placed in a single grave, one laid directly above the other. Babies were buried in the floors of the houses— so that their nearness, perhaps, might give the mothers some small comfort. So many Yuchi infants died soon after birth that they were considered half-spirit and half-human for the first four days. During these critical days, while the child was still linked to the spirit world, it was neither suckled nor clothed. Since they believed in reincarnation, the Yuchi thought that the spirit of an ancestor entered the body of a newborn baby during its first few days of life. On the fourth day, if the child survived, it was given a name, often that of the ancestor whose spirit, it was hoped, had

CRUDE ANIMAL EFFIGIES MADE BY MEN

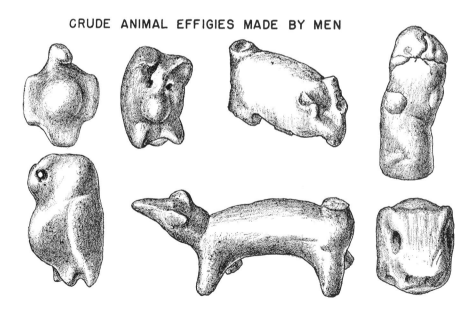

returned. In token of having a name, a string of small white beads was tied around the infant's neck. Hence, when the small skeletons are found without beads, it may be inferred that the child died before it was four days old.

The Yuchi believed that every person had four spirits. At death, one of the spirits continued to hover around the home, two others remained in the neighborhood of the tribe, while the fourth departed for heaven. This wandering spirit was obliged to travel four days on the path of the rainbow before reaching its destination.

Occasionally, upon the death of a prominent person, a special coffin was made from thin slabs of stone instead of bark. Owing to the scarcity of suitable rock near the Yuchi towns in eastern Tennessee, it was seldom used. But in Middle Tennessee where thin layers of limestone, slate and shale are abundant, stone coffins were common. They were long and narrow, exactly like the graves in the Yuchi towns. Not only were the graves the same shape, but the corpses were laid out in the identical position. Yet there was a slight difference. The Middle Tennessee Indians usually had special cemeteries for their dead, while the East Tennessee Yuchi often buried them close to the houses or in the house floors, although in some cases an area in the village was reserved for graves. The cemeteries of old Middle Tennessee towns sometimes contain tier upon tier of stone coffins and appear as mounds. In that area, the custom of burying two bodies at the

DOUBLE BURIAL

same time in a single coffin was also practiced occasionally, and graves opened and reused. In such instances, the first occupant's bones were shoved to one end so that the new corpse could be stretched out in the proper burial position.

Stone slab coffins were sporadically used by people who, like the Creeks, buried the dead in partly folded positions, but then the coffins were made shorter and wider, or even circular in shape. The stone slab coffin idea was apparently borrowed by many tribes and therefore it cannot be used by itself to identify any particular group. The custom may have originated in Middle Tennessee, inspired partly by the natural formations of limestone slabs and partly by the thinness of the soil which allowed for only very shallow graves to be dug. Certainly, such graves are far more numerous there than anywhere else in the eastern United States, and most of them were associated with temple mound cultures.

Whether Middle Tennessee was the earlier home of the Yuchi cannot be definitely proved, yet many things lead to this belief. By the time the Yuchi had established towns in eastern Tennessee, their culture had been so modified by contact with both the Creeks and the Cherokee that similarities are generalized rather than specific.

STONE SLAB COFFIN

The men of the Yuchi tribe were organized into two large groupings, the Chiefs' Society and the Warriors' Society. The Chiefs' Society included the officials who had charge of civil and religious affairs, hence it was the peace organization and conducted the religious ceremonies. In addition to furnishing the head chief and four chiefs in charge of ceremonies for each town, the society also provided the medicine men.

The Warriors' Society paralleled the Chiefs' Society in organization, since it had a head war chief and four assistants. Much less is known about Yuchi war customs than about those of the Creeks, Cherokees and other southern Indians. By reputation they were fierce and fearless, but their towns were too scattered after 1714 for them to retain a functioning military organization, except as a part of the Creek confederacy whose customs eventually largely replaced their own.

Although the identifiable Yuchi culture is Mississippian in type, they did not build temple mounds in eastern Tennessee. This may be accounted for by the fact that the Yuchi towns had scarcely been inhabited long enough for mounds to have been constructed. Furthermore, the custom of rebuilding temple mounds was apparently abandoned by all of the Indian groups in the 1700's when the fur trade began to absorb much of their time and energy. And later, when the tribes became pawns of the European nations in their rivalry for colonial empires, warfare instigated by the Europeans left little time for public works in Indian towns.

The ultimate fate of the Yuchi, like the Creeks, was removal to Indian Territory in the early eighteenth century. By 1930, census returns showed only 216 Yuchi still surviving.

Chapter 9

"Principal People"

RIGHT-HAND MAN   CHEROKEE CHIEF   SPEAKER

DႹ BႧႡ

A NI   YUN WI YA

PEOPLE   PRINCIPAL

THE SEVEN CHEROKEE CLANS

DႹ ႦWⵏႧ

A NI GA TO GE WI

WILD POTATO

DႹ ⵏⴰⵡⵣ

A NI   TSI   S KWA

BIRD

DႹ ႯႩჄ

A NI   GI LO HI

LONG HAIR

DႹ ႮႠႦ

A NI   SA HO NI

BLUE

DႹ ႭႩⵣ

A NI   WO DI

PAINT

DႹ ႧႧ

A NI   KA WI

DEER

DႹ GႡ

A NI   WA YAH

WOLF

"Principal People"

With some justification the Cherokee called themselves *Ani-Yunwiya,* which in their language means "Principal People." They formed the largest single tribe in the South, and one of the largest of all tribes north of Mexico. With an estimated population of 22,000 in 1650, they numbered more than 45,000 in the 1930 census. Although they never occupied more than a small part of Tennessee in either prehistoric or historic times, they had a strong influence on the area and its people, both Indian and white.

The Cherokee are not easily identified with any of the prehistoric cultures of the Southeast. Their own migration legends have often been misunderstood and have been interpreted to mean that they did not settle in the South until rather late in prehistoric times. But Indian migration legends generally tend to telescope time, because they have been handed down by word of mouth and use figures of speech that are difficult to translate accurately. Furthermore, most historical accounts that have been handed down in that manner stress dramatic and crucial events and ignore the long, uneventful decades that intervene between them.

The Cherokee once had a dim tradition of their ancestors having come to North America as part of a long, drawn-out, mass migration in which the Delawares, an Algonkin tribe, formed the vanguard. Because of this leadership, Cherokee tradition says that the Delawares were the grandfathers of all the Indians, and that they (the Cherokee) were uncles of the Creeks, Choctaws and Chickasaws, and brothers to certain other tribes. The other tribes were undoubtedly the Iroquois and Tuscaroras who spoke languages related to Cherokee. The tradition further recounts that just before or just after crossing a great body of water, the tribes separated, some going south and others going north.

The Cherokee language, which is related to Iroquois, is so dissimilar from Iroquois that linguists believe that the two peoples have been separated for a very long time. The fact, however, that basic similarities do exist is evidence that both languages descended from a common tongue. From this it may be assumed that the Cherokee and the Iroquois were once a single people who separated from each other in the distant past.

There is some evidence from archaeology that the Cherokee were long-time inhabitants of the Southeast. Their older town sites reveal that stamped decoration on pottery was a part of their culture from the earliest times. Whether or not they were among the first southeastern Indians to develop this art, it was firmly entrenched in their culture and persisted until the twentieth century, long after other groups had abandoned it.

But what of the name "Cherokee," the one by which these Indians have been known throughout the historic period? The first use of this was probably in the De Soto narratives where it appeared as Achelaque, the name of a province near the mountains visited by De Soto in 1540. The derivation may be from the Muskhogean word *tciloki* meaning "people who speak a different language." Since the Indian guides of the De Soto expedition were Muskhogean, they probably used the common Muskhogean term *tciloki* in referring to the population of the mountain region. At any rate, the name seems to have stuck, because it appears in Spanish, French and English colonial records (with many variations in spelling, to be sure), and even the Cherokee themselves adopted it in the form of *Tsalagi.*

While early Cherokee culture may have belonged to the Woodland tradition, the late prehistoric Cherokee culture was essentially Mississippian. The processes by which this evolution in culture took place included both acculturation through borrowing and internal development.

The dawn of the historic period found the Cherokee living in about eighty towns that were distributed among four large groups as follows:

1. The Middle settlements, or the heart of the nation, centering in North Carolina on the headwaters of the Tuckaseegee and Little Tennessee rivers.
2. The Valley settlements, also in North Carolina, along the Valley, Nottely and upper Hiwassee rivers.
3. The Lower settlements on the Tugaloo River in northern Georgia and Keowee River in South Carolina.
4. The Overhill settlements in Tennessee, with a few towns along the middle portion of the Hiwassee River, a few on the Tellico River, but the majority along the Little Tennessee River.

Three different Cherokee dialects were spoken: the one used in the Lower settlements is now extinct; the one used in the Middle settlements is still spoken on the Qualla Reservation in the Smoky Mountains; and the one used in the Valley and Overhill settlements is spoken on the Cherokee Reservation in Oklahoma. The differences in the dialects were mainly in pronunciation, rather than in vocabulary.

The whole Cherokee nation was organized under a principal chief, but settlement groups functioned as the units of political, military and religious life, except in great emergencies or for special national ceremonies.

The Cherokee towns varied in size from a dozen up to two hundred dwellings, the average being about one hundred. In the center of each town was an open square for dances and ceremonies. On the west side of the square stood the council house or temple, and around the square and council house were grouped the dwellings and gardens. Towns on the borders were often fortified with stockades whose gates were guarded day and night.

Each family had a house built similarly to those of other Mississippian Indians. A small, scooped-out fireplace occupied the center of the floor, and beside it was a large, flat hearthstone for baking corn bread. One end of the house was used for storage of food and other family possessions, and the other end for sleeping. The beds, arranged around the walls at that end, were made of saplings and woven splints. This type of house furnished the main living quarters, but each family also had a smaller, partly subterranean, winter house where the members slept during cold weather. The winter house was furnished with beds and had a fireplace where a fire was kept burning all day, and banked at night. The white traders, who called these "hot houses," borrowed the idea and built similar ones for their own comfort.

Hot houses were used by medicine men for giving sweat baths, a standard method of treating certain diseases, as well as a purification ritual. Still another use for the hot houses was for secret meetings where certain priests, called "Myth Keepers," recited and discussed the lore of the tribe, and instructed chosen young men in the secret knowledge of myth keepers.

The Cherokee council house was a combination temple for religious rites and public hall for civil and military councils, hence it had both sacred and secular features, with the sacred predominating. The traditional council house was seven-sided and could seat as many as five hundred persons. The seven sides corresponded to the seven clans of the Cherokee, with the members of each clan being seated in its designated section.

The main framework of the council house was also based upon the sacred number seven. Seven large upright pillars, spaced equidistant, outlined the outer walls, and within were two more concentric series of seven posts and a single large central pillar. Three tiers of benches around the walls were elevated to form an amphitheatre. The entrance, which was on the east side of the building, faced the square ground, but was constructed as a winding corridor to prevent the interior from being seen from outside. Opposite the door at the west side of the building was the sacred area where all of the ceremonial costumes and paraphernalia were kept. This area was determined by the large pillar of the outer wall which was known as the sacred

CORN GRINDING

seventh pillar. In this area of the council house were seated all of the main officials, three of whom had special seats with high carved backs. These seats were whitened with a mixture of clay, white being symbolic of purity and sacredness. Near the central post, and in front of the officials' seats, was the altar where a perpetual fire burned. During war councils, three additional seats for war leaders were installed in front of those for the three civil officials. These were similar to the others, but painted red to symbolize war.

The Cherokee, like the rest of the southern Indians in the late prehistoric period, were farmers, although they were obliged to hunt in order to obtain their meat. Corn was their main crop, but they also grew beans, gourds, pumpkins and sunflowers, the seeds of the latter being ground into flour. Three varieties of corn were grown: "six weeks corn," a small type like popcorn that ripened in about two months and was roasted in the milk stage; "hominy corn" with smooth, hard kernels that might be red, blue, white, yellow, or any combinations of these colors; and finally "flour corn" which was the most important and had very large, white kernels.

Corn, being literally the staff of life to the Cherokee, was the subject of myths and ritual. At every stage of its cultivation and harvesting, ceremonies and magical rites were performed to insure its welfare. The common name for corn was *tsalu*, but the name for the spirit of corn was *Agawela*, which meant "Old Woman." The latter name came from the Cherokee legend about the origin of corn from the body of a woman who was killed by her own sons.

Besides the cultivated plant foods and game, the Cherokee made great use of nuts, wild fruits, roots, mushrooms, fish, crayfish, frogs, birds' eggs, and even yellow jacket grubs and cicadas. Food was often scarce in the spring before the new crops were ready to eat, and survival depended upon utilizing everything edible in the environment.

The old Cherokee crafts were similar to those of the other

southern Indians. Stone pipes, however, were a specialty. These were skillfully carved in the shapes of birds and animals, and occasionally in human form. Many of them, massive affairs weighing several pounds, were ceremonial pipes used only at council meetings. The Smoky Mountains furnished the pipestone, a greenish steatite, that was readily carved with flint knives.

Wood carving was another distinctive Cherokee craft. Intricate geometrical designs were carved on the wooden pottery paddles and on long, wooden pipestems. Dance masks were examples of three-dimensional wood sculpture, and drums hollowed out of buckeye were decorated with low relief carvings of animals. Many objects of everyday use were carved from wood, including huge dugout canoes. These were made from poplar trees that were hollowed out by alternate burning and scraping. Although the canoes were thirty to forty feet long, they were not excessively heavy or clumsy. The width was about two feet and the depth about one foot, with the thickness of the wood vary-

MAKING A DUGOUT

ing from one to two inches.

An important Cherokee weapon was the blowgun. It was about eight feet long and made from hollowed-out cane. Small, slender wooden darts, tufted with thistledown, were blown with enough force to kill small game and birds. While several other southern Indian groups used blowguns, those of the Cherokee were unusually well made and accurate.

The Cherokee excelled in weaving baskets and mats from narrow strips of cane dyed in several brilliant colors with native vegetable dyes. Intricate patterns were achieved with various combinations of colors and weaves. Some of the finest examples of Indian weaving are the double woven Cherokee baskets, made in the early historical period, that have been preserved in museums.

Garments made of feathers were both beautiful and practical —practical because they were warm without being heavy and bulky like those made from skins. The feathers came from the breasts of wild turkeys and were about two or three inches long. They were sewed between narrow strips of bark, and the strips were then sewed together so that the feathers overlapped as on the body of the turkey. Skirts for women and mantles for both sexes were made in this manner. Feathers from brilliantly colored

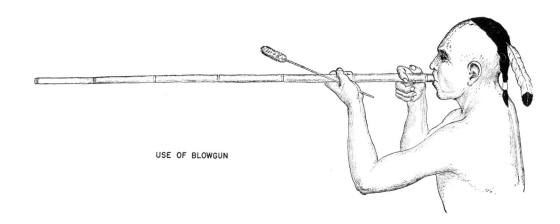

USE OF BLOWGUN

birds were worked into these garments as trimmings. Feathers of other kinds, particularly those from eagles and white cranes, were used in headdresses.

The patterns of clothing were simple, the women wearing short skirts and shoulder mantles, and the men, breech clouts and sleeveless shirts. Both sexes wore moccasins that were made like short boots and reached halfway up the leg. While they were on hunting trips in the forest and in cold weather, men wore leather leggings like loose trouser legs.

Cherokee society had a number of institutions. First, there was the family in which maternal descent was emphasized. This was closely linked to the clan organization, because all children belonged to the clan of their mother, and each generation in the

WEAVING BASKET WITH SPLIT CANE

clan considered themselves to be brothers and sisters. Within the family, inheritance of position, privileges and prerogatives passed from the mother's brother to the nephews. Relationship on the father's side was also recognized, but was less intimate. Every individual had closer relationships with four of the seven clans than with the other three, the four being: the mother's clan, of which the person was also a member; the father's clan; the paternal grandfather's (father's father's) clan; and the maternal grandfather's (mother's father's) clan. These last two were important because a person was expected to marry into one or the other. In any single town, all of the seven clans were represented; this prevailed throughout the nation and linked all of the Cherokee by kinship bonds. However, there were other allegiances as well.

Each town and every settlement group had its own civil, religious and military organizations which, although less elaborate, paralleled those of the national institutions. At the head of the nation was a paramount chief who was selected for his wisdom, integrity and ability as a leader. He was not only the head of all civil affairs, but also the religious head. He had two assistants, his right-hand man and his speaker, who sat at either side of him on the three white seats in the council house. In addition, there were five other advisors who, with the first two, made up a council of seven. A number of minor officials performed specific tasks at council meetings and ceremonies. Some of these were priests and medicine men, rather than strictly governmental officers, yet their functions were indispensable at all council meetings.

The military organization was separate and consisted of a chief warrior, three main officers and seven counselors. Special medicine men were assigned to the war organization, their duties being a combination of magic, fortune telling, practical surgery, and spiritual solace.

The chief warrior had two titles, "Greatly Honored Man" and "The Raven," the latter title coming from his insignia of office, a raven's skin. This hung around his neck, with the raven's head on his breast and the wings draped around his shoulders and tied in the back. His entire costume and all of his weapons were dyed blood-red, except for the raven skin and an eagle feather tied to his scalp lock. Although the chief warrior had to be courageous and take the lead in battle, his wisdom and ability to control men were equally important qualifications. At his consecration as war chief, he was required to take an oath never to go to war without just cause and never to shed the blood of infants, women, old men, or any person unable to defend himself.

Women played an important role in war, particularly one woman whose title, *Agiyagustu,* meant "Honored Woman." Often called the "War Woman" by the white men, she sat with the council and had a vote in deciding whether or not war would be declared. She also had the power of life or death over captives—death by torture, or life as an adopted member of the tribe. If she decided that the captive should be saved, one of the head women of the clans was required to adopt the person into her family and clan. The last "Honored Woman" was Nancy Ward who often warned white settlers of attacks and was known to have saved one Tennessee white woman from being burned at the stake.

The capital of the nation changed according to the residence of the paramount chief. In 1715 it was at Tugaloo in the Lower settlements in northeastern Georgia; by 1730 it had shifted to Chote on the Little Tennessee River in Tennessee. Chote continued to be the capital until the town was finally abandoned and the national organization revised.

The religious organization of the Cherokee was closely interrelated with the civil government. All persons who held the main governmental positions were dedicated in childhood and underwent special training. This was the same training that the various classes of medicine men received. They were educated during periods of fasting and had regular instruction in the traditional history, religious beliefs, rituals and sacred medicinal formulas.

Dances, which formed part of Cherokee religious ceremonies, were also performed before going to war, to celebrate the return of victorious warriors, to greet visitors, and for recreation. The dance figures were always circular in motion, usually counter-clockwise. They were accompanied by drums, flutes, rattles and singing. Gourd rattles were carried in the hand by men, while turtle shell rattles filled with small pebbles were worn by women on their lower legs.

The eagle dance was for celebrating victories, and also for symbolizing peace when visitors were greeted. The eagle feather fans carried by the dancers were made of the long, white tail feathers of the golden eagle. These feathers were so highly valued that only certain hunters, versed in the proper rituals, could procure them. The feather fans were carried in the left hands of women and in the right hands of men, the men holding gourd rattles in their left hands. To stumble during the dance, or to allow the fan to touch the ground, was considered unlucky and likely to cause early death.

The warrior dance was performed before a war party set out, and by men only. Each warrior carried a ceremonial war club painted red and black, red symbolizing blood and black indicating fearlessness. The dance began slowly, then gained in tempo as the warriors pretended to strike the enemy with their clubs, and finally finished with four loud war whoops.

Many of the social dances were named after animals and birds, the dance figures pantomiming either the hunting of the creatures or some characteristic behavior, as for example, the mating dance of partridges. Most of these dances were humorous and provided one of the main sources of recreation. All-night dance sessions were popular and were community affairs in which everyone took part. Besides affording diversion, these sessions promoted social bonds by bringing everyone together. Social dancing usually followed the great religious festivals during which all the population of a settlement group gathered in one main town.

The foregoing is a description of Cherokee culture before the white men disrupted the pattern. Indian life was by no means entirely peaceful in pre-Columbian times. Intertribal warfare, however, was a matter of hit-and-run raids against hereditary enemies, rather than wars of conquest and extermination. The Cherokee were inveterate enemies of the Creeks, Shawnee, Iroquois, Catawba, Yuchi and Delawares, but in their relationships with these tribes, periods of hostility alternated with interludes of peace. The custom of adopting captives that prevailed among most of the Indians of eastern North America was an important factor in leveling cultural distinctions. With the advent of white men and the introduction of imperialistic colonialism, the Indians experienced a new type of international relations—one which resulted finally in complete eviction from their homelands, and almost in their liquidation as a racial and cultural entity.

The gradual eviction of the Cherokee began in 1721, with a treaty ceding a tract of land in South Carolina. The Cherokee and the other eastern tribes had become cat's-paws of the English and French in their rivalries for control of the territory and resources of the New World. Sweeping concessions were made to the English in 1730 when six prominent men of the Cherokee nation visited England and there concluded a treaty. In this treaty they conceded to the English exclusive rights to trade and build forts in their territory.

The French and Indian War that actually began in 1754, two years before it was formally declared, was a period that strained British-Cherokee relationships to the breaking point. The French, who had followed a policy of encircling the struggling English colonies, were firmly entrenched in the Mississippi Valley and had gained a strong southeastern vantage point by establishing Fort Toulouse near Montgomery, Alabama. Only the Cherokee among the southern Indians remained friendly to the English, but they were wavering until the colony of South Carolina agreed to build a fort in the Overhill region. It was named Fort Loudoun in honor of the Earl of Loudoun, Commander in Chief of the British forces in North America.

The purpose of Fort Loudoun was to protect the women, children and aged while the Cherokee warriors accompanied colonial troops on expeditions against the French in the Ohio Valley. During such expeditions, the Overhill towns were left undefended against the Indian allies of the French. The fort, built during the winter and spring of 1756–1757 on the Little Tennessee River, was a lone outpost west of the Appalachians, yet its diplomatic and strategic significance far outweighed its military strength. It ensured the friendship of the Cherokee and stabilized the southern frontier during the crucial year of 1758 when the Ohio Valley was a focus of British-French conflict. But even while Cherokee warriors accompanied young Colonel George Washington on his successful expedition against Fort Du Quesne, the seeds of distrust were sown.

In 1759, provoked by French subversive influence and by conflicts with English settlers, war broke out between the Cherokee and the British. Fort Loudoun was besieged in 1760, and the garrison, after six months of desperate defense, was forced to surrender. Although the Cherokee had agreed to allow the soldiers to return unmolested to South Carolina, they attacked the defeated and disarmed troops on the second day after the evacuation of the fort. With one exception, all of the officers and

FORT LOUDOUN

twenty or more of the men were killed on the spot. The rest were taken captive, and for some of them this fate was worse than sudden death; they were subjected to painful, lingering deaths by torture. Those who survived were eventually ransomed.

After the defeat of the Cherokee in 1761 and the end of the French and Indian War in 1763, land hungry settlers from the coast poured into the valleys of eastern Tennessee. Within twelve years, constant land cessions reduced the Cherokee territories to a mere fraction of their former extent. Another fifty years were to see the Indians almost completely dispossessed of their homeland.

When the Revolutionary War broke out, the Cherokee took the side of the Crown against the American settlers, with the result that they not only were on the losing side, but by 1791 had been forced to cede practically all the land east of the mountains, plus much of eastern Tennessee.

The end of the eighteenth century found about 20,000 Cherokee still living on their reduced lands and gradually taking over the white man's culture. Many of the early traders had married Cherokee women, and the mixed offspring of these marriages became very influential in the Cherokee nation. A number of them were far better educated and had a higher standard of living than the rank and file of white settlers. Schools and missions were established, and by 1820 the Cherokee adopted a republican form of government with a president and a legislature having an upper and lower house. Eight years later, the publication of a national newspaper began, the *Cherokee Phoenix,* which was printed both in Cherokee and English.

Back of the story of the newspaper is the story of the best known Cherokee Indian, Sequoyah. Sequoyah's real name was George Gist. He was the son of Nathaniel Gist from Virginia and a Cherokee woman, sister of the principal chief. He was born about the middle of the eighteenth century in one of the Overhill towns. As a young man he was an accomplished silversmith and became quite famous for his work.

By the end of the eighteenth century, some of the Cherokee,

especially the offspring of mixed marriages, had learned to read and write. Sequoyah, although he never learned to read or write English, was fascinated by the idea that a person could make marks on paper and communicate his exact ideas to another person miles away. He was convinced that this could be done with the Cherokee language, and, in spite of being thought a fool by his friends and family, he dedicated himself to the task.

His first step was an attempt to devise signs for complete sentences, but he soon gave that up. Next, he tried to make signs for words, and again found that his idea was impractical. Finally, he hit upon the idea of breaking words into syllables, and discovered that eighty-six signs were sufficient to render all of the sound combinations in the Cherokee language. Apparently, he had access to some German printed characters, possibly through Moravian missionaries who established a mission among the Cherokee in 1801. Later, he copied letters out of a Bible which he saw during a visit at the home of his brother-in-law. With a few basic symbols which he modified by turning them in different directions and by adding various strokes and curlicues, plus other symbols which he invented, he created the Cherokee alphabet, or more properly, syllabary.

After he demonstrated in 1821 to the leading men of the nation that his invention was practical, Sequoyah soon became one of the most honored men in the nation. Within a few months after the acceptance of the alphabet, almost the entire Cherokee nation became literate. This led to the establishment of the newspaper that was published for a number of years until agitation for removal of all of the Indians to the West resulted in acts of violence, among which were the destruction of the presses and the arrest of the printer.

The climax of the tribulations of the Cherokee was the infamous treaty of New Echota in 1835, engineered by the federal government of the United States. By this the Cherokee were to cede all of their eastern lands and to emigrate west of the Mississippi River. The treaty was signed by a small group of Indians, but by none of the officers of the Cherokee nation.

Efforts to revoke the treaty, both on the part of the Cherokee and prominent white leaders (among whom were Henry Clay, Daniel Webster and David Crockett), failed. In 1838 the forcible expatriation, known to the Cherokee as the "trail of tears," began. Some thirteen thousand Cherokee were rounded up into concentration camps to await deportation. In October, 1838 at the onset of winter, the exiles began the long march, most of them on foot. Winter overtook them on the trail. Suffering from the effects of cold, insufficient food, exhaustion and disease, thousands died along the way, including the wife of the beloved principal chief, John Ross.

The problems of the Cherokee did not end with the removal. As early as 1817, many Cherokee had migrated of their own voli-

ON THE "TRAIL OF TEARS"

tion to Arkansas and had become well established. At first they welcomed the ten thousand or so exiles who survived the "trail of tears," but soon frictions developed. The old settlers had an organized government and objected to being swallowed up by the newcomers. After some months of bitter quarrels, the two parts of the nation reunited, but disputes between various factions continued for a generation.

When the Civil War broke out, sentiment among the Cherokee was divided, one faction favoring the Confederacy, another the Union, and a third determined on strict neutrality. Although they finally concluded a treaty with the Confederacy, thousands favored the Union. As a result of guerrilla warfare between internal factions, and the raids by both Confederate and Union forces, the Cherokee country was ravaged for five years, and a third of the population died.

Slowly during the next twenty years the nation rebuilt its homes, schools and churches, and again became prosperous, only to discover that its independence was finally to be destroyed. By the beginning of the twentieth century the Cherokee and other independent Indian nations were reduced to reservation tribes under federal government agents.

The small group of Cherokee who still remain on the Qualla Reservation in North Carolina are descended from somewhat over a thousand refugees who hid in the mountains during the roundup of 1838. Due to the intercession of Colonel William Thomas, a trader for many years among the Cherokee, and the sacrifice of Tsali who gave his own life and the lives of his two oldest sons, the fugitives were allowed to remain. They now number about three thousand, of which about one-third are full Cherokee. They are citizens of North Carolina, but maintain their own government which consists of an elected council and chief. Conscious and proud of their own heritage, the eastern Cherokee are one of the few Indian peoples east of the Mississippi who still live in their native homeland.

Chapter 10
The Sacred Seven

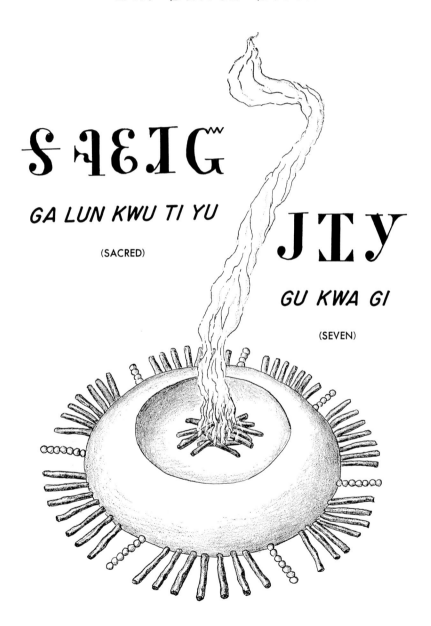

GA LUN KWU TI YU

(SACRED)

GU KWA GI

(SEVEN)

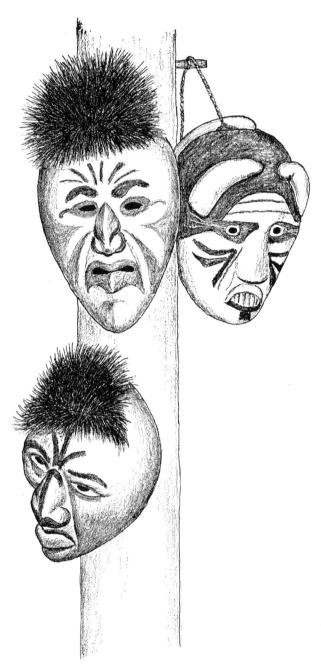

CARVED WOODEN DANCE MASKS

The Sacred Seven

Sacred numbers are present in the beliefs of most of the peoples of the world, and the ancient Cherokee were no exception. For them, the number was seven, and it pervaded nearly all aspects of their lives. Even their conception of the Universe was sevenfold, with seven heavens and seven directions—north, south, east, west, above, below, and "here in the center." Seven clans were the foundation of their social organization, and seven great ceremonies formed the cycle of their religious life.

Belief in one supreme being formed the central theme of their religion. This being's name was *Yowa*, a name so sacred that it could not be spoken aloud, except by certain priests. Even such individuals, dedicated from childhood to the performance of religious rites, uttered it in public only while singing a hymn—a hymn that was sung but once a year.

Yowa, the supreme god, was conceived of as a unity of three beings, referred to as "The Elder Fires Above," who were the creators of the universe. These Elder Fires first created the sun and the moon and gave the world its form. Then they returned to the seventh heaven in the sky, leaving the sun and the moon to finish the creation of the stars and all living things, and to rule over them. This explains why Cherokee prayers used the expression, "Sun, my creator."

During the process of creation, the sun and the moon appointed fire to be the protector of human beings and to be the intermediary between man and the sun. Smoke was the fire's messenger who bore the prayers of man from earth to heaven.

The moon deity controlled Cherokee religious rituals, its crescent or new moon phase establishing the dates for ceremonies. The Cherokee believed that the world was created in the autumn season when the fruits were ripe. Hence their year began when the new moon of October appeared.

Other supernatural beings were prominent in the religion and mythology of the Cherokee. There were spirits to symbolize the four directions to which special qualities were attributed. East was a red spirit whose significance was power in war, North was a blue spirit signifying defeat, West was the black specter of death, and South, the white spirit of peace. Most things in nature were believed to have spirit counterparts—thunder, animals, plants, water, etc. And the mountains and forests were peopled with fairies who were friendly when undisturbed, but mischievous when offended. Then there were ghosts, the spirits of the dead that hovered around their former homes before finally departing for the other world and its seven heavens.

The sacredness of the number seven was constantly emphasized in Cherokee ceremonies. Six of these took place each year, but the seventh was celebrated only every seven years. They were held at the capital town of the nation where the paramount chief resided, and the local inhabitants welcomed into their homes the visitors who congregated from far and wide. In preparation, messengers were dispatched throughout the nation to announce the date in advance, and hunters from the capital town sent to the forests to seek meat for the feasts. The six annual ceremonies, which took place between March and November, will be described in the order of their occurrence.

First New Moon of Spring

When the grass began to grow and the trees send out their pale new leaves, the chief and his advisors met to plan for the festival in honor of the first new moon of spring. At this meeting, held early in March during the dark of the moon, seven elder women, honored leaders in their respective clans, performed the Friendship Dance. Then the chief, after conferring with his advisors, announced the date of the ceremony and ordered the messengers to notify the towns in the nation. During the following days, while some of the men went hunting, others repaired the altar in the temple and procured firewood from seven different species of trees.

On the day set by the chief, the visitors from all of the other towns assembled at the capital. When evening came and the moon's slender crescent appeared above the western horizon, the women opened the ceremony with the Friendship Dance. By the time the dance was finished, the moon had set, and the first day's activities were over.

Shortly after dawn the next morning, the entire population crowded into the temple. The chief, now acting as high priest, brought out the sacred crystal which was believed to have the power to foretell the future. Pure quartz crystals, used by Cherokee chiefs and priests on most important occasions, were considered peculiarly sacred, and at the same time dangerous—only persons trained from childhood could handle them without harmful effects. Because this festival initiated the planting season, the crystal's predictions were concerned with the success or failure of the crops. The people awaited these predictions, tense with emotion compounded of hope and anxiety.

After this part of the ritual, everyone left the temple and assembled on the river bank. There, they plunged into the water and, facing toward the east, completely submerged themselves seven times. Following this chilly purification, they changed into dry clothes to await the feast which would take place after sunset. Because no food had been eaten since the day before, it may be imagined that these hours seemed very long.

Just before sunset, everyone returned to the temple where the

priest performed a ritual sacrifice by burning dried tobacco flowers and a deer's tongue in the sacred fire. The smoke from this
sacrifice was believed to carry the prayers of the Cherokee to the
sun. The feast followed this rite, and after the feast the night was
spent in dancing.

Seven days later, the interim being a period for visiting and
recreation, the people again met in the temple, this time for the

THE CRYSTAL GAZER

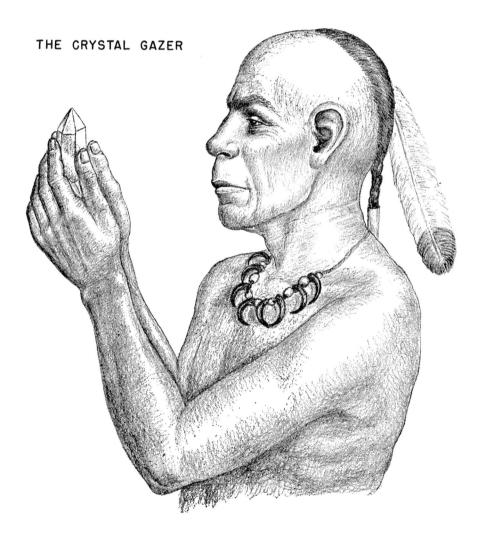

ritual of relighting the sacred fire. The fire-maker, a person initiated into the mysteries of the tribal religion, extinguished the altar flames and, with the aid of his six assistants, prepared to rekindle it. For this, he used two pieces of dry basswood, one a rod and the other a flat slab having a cup-shaped depression. Placing some tinder composed of dried goldenrod blossoms in the depression, he rotated the rod rapidly back and forth between the palms of his hands until the friction produced fire. Once the tinder was ignited, the feeble flame was fed with the seven different kinds of wood. Previously, the fires in the homes had been extin-

KINDLING THE SACRED FIRE

guished, and all of the old ashes removed from the hearths. After the sacred fire in the temple was once more burning strongly, the women were given glowing coals to relight their hearth fires. Even the visitors carried home burning embers to be used for the same purpose.

Green Corn Ceremony

In August when the new corn crop was ripe enough to eat, the Green Corn Ceremony took place, eating of new corn being tabooed until after this event. Preliminary preparations were the same as for the first new moon of spring festival, except that along the route the messengers gathered seven ears of corn, each of these ears coming from a field of a different clan. When the messengers returned with the corn, the chief and his seven counselors fasted for the following six days. Meanwhile, the people assembled, and after an all night vigil, the ceremony began on the seventh day.

The sacred fire was extinguished and rekindled as before, and the chief prepared the sacrifice. In addition to the deer's tongue, he used kernels from each of seven ears of corn. First he dedicated the corn to *Yowa* and offered a prayer of thanksgiving. Then, placing the corn and the deer's tongue in the sacred fire, he sprinkled over them a powder made from tobacco.

In the meantime, food prepared from the new corn was brought to the temple where everyone was served—that is, everyone except the chief and his seven counselors who for another seven days could only eat corn from the previous year's harvest.

Ripe Corn Ceremony

Only one of all the ancient ceremonies of the Cherokee survived until the twentieth century. It was primarily a harvest festival to celebrate the final maturing of the corn crop. Since it lacked many of the religious features of the other ceremonies, conflict was less between it and doctrines of the Christian religion which the Cherokee began to adopt during the eighteenth century.

In late September, the usual preparations for notifying the nation and providing food for the feasts having begun, the square ground was made ready. The ceremony was an outdoor affair lasting four days, during which feasting and dancing were the main activities. Arbors shaded by boughs were constructed around the square, and a leafy tree was set in the center. A special portable platform, upon which the right-hand man of the chief was to perform a dance, was also built. Each man then provided himself with a green bough to be carried during the men's dance.

This dance was performed during the daytime and, while it was taking place, women were excluded from the square. The dance started some distance beyond the square, each man carrying his green bough in his right hand. As they followed a leader in single file, the men entered the square and circled the tree in the center seven times, singing and leaping in the traditional steps of the dance. Meanwhile, on the platform held aloft on the shoulders of a group of men, the chief's right-hand man performed his dance. During each of the four days of the ceremony, the men carried out this ritual which was one of intense exertion and excitement. After sunset came the feast which was followed by social dances in the square, women also participating in these.

Many of the elder Cherokee, still living on the Qualla Reservation in western North Carolina, remember the modified version of this ceremony in which they took part during their youth. Even today the Cherokee Indian Fair dimly echoes the ancient harvest home festival of the ripe corn, for it is the great annual social event at Qualla.

Great New Moon Ceremony

When autumn leaves began to fall and the October new moon appeared in the sky, the new year ceremony took place. This was the season of the year in which the world was created, ac-

cording to Cherokee tradition. The proper name for the ceremony was *Nuwatiegwa,* meaning "big medicine," but it was also
called the Great New Moon Ceremony.

In addition to the usual preparations, each family that at-
tended brought produce from its own fields—corn, beans, pumpkins, etc. Part of this was for the general feast and the rest for
the chief to distribute among unfortunate families whose harvest
had been insufficient.

On the night of the moon's appearance, the women performed
a religious dance. Only infants were permitted to sleep, the rest
of the people keeping vigil until just before dawn. Then everyone, infants included, assembled on the river bank and were
arranged in one long line by the priest. At sunrise the priest sig-
naled for all to wade in and submerge themselves and their children seven times. While this was taking place, the priest placed
the sacred crystal on a stand near the river's edge. Then, emerg-
ing from the water, one at a time, the people gazed into the crystal. If their image reflected by the crystal appeared to be lying
down, they believed that they would die before spring. If, on the
other hand, they appeared to be standing erect, they would survive the coming winter.

Those who felt themselves doomed remained apart and
fasted, while the others changed into dry clothes and returned
to the temple. There the priest made the usual sacrifice of a deer's
tongue, and a feast followed. Most of the night was devoted to
a religious dance by the women, and none but infants slept.

Before nightfall, those who had seen themselves lying down in
the crystal were taken once more by the priest to the river bank
where the crystal-gazing was repeated. If on the second try, some
saw themselves standing erect, they repeated the seven sub-
mergings in the river and then considered themselves safe. The
unfortunates, whose images on the second try were still reclining,
had one more chance to escape their fate. But this was deferred
until the next new moon, four weeks later.

This was a short ceremony lasting only two days and nights. It was followed after ten days by the fifth ceremony, the intervening time being devoted to preparations.

Reconciliation or "Friends Made" Ceremony

Atohuna, meaning "friends made," was the name of the fifth ceremony. The name referred to a relationship between two persons of either the same or opposite sex. This relationship was a bond of eternal friendship in which each person vowed to regard the other as himself as long as they both lived. The guiding theme of the ceremony was a universal vow of brotherly love, and entailed reconciliation between those who had quarreled during the previous year. Beyond its earthly significance, the ceremony symbolized the uniting of the people with *Yowa,* and a purification of their minds and bodies. Hence, of all the Cherokee ceremonies it was the most profoundly religious.

During the ten days that intervened between this and the Great New Moon Ceremony, seven hunters were sent after game, seven other men to procure seven kinds of evergreen plants, and seven more to clean and prepare the temple. In addition, seven women were designated to fast for seven days in company with the chief officials.

Just before dawn on the day of the ceremony, the sacred vessels and the seats for the officials were whitened with clay. White buckskins were spread over the seats and on the ground in front of them, white being symbolic of peace and purity.

At sunrise, the people assembled in the temple to witness the ritual rekindling of the sacred fire. Seven different kinds of wood —blackjack oak, post oak, red oak, sycamore, locust, plum and redbud—were used to feed the fire. Next, the high priest sprinkled powdered tobacco on the fire, and as the smoke rose, he wafted it in the four cardinal directions, using the wing of a white heron as a fan. Then a whitened pottery vessel filled with water was placed on the fire, and a small cane basket containing the seven evergreen plants was dropped into it. This brew, composed of cedar, white pine, hemlock, mistletoe, greenbrier, heart leaf and ginseng, became the ritual medicine of purification that was used on several occasions during the five days of the festival.

The second event of the ceremony was performed by seven men furnished with white sycamore rods. Their function was to drive away evil spirits by chanting a sacred formula while they struck the eaves of all buildings with their rods. While they were carrying out this task, the priest who was to sing the great hymn to *Yowa* was dressed in white robes by his assistants. When the men with the sycamore rods returned, he went outside and began to sing, ascending onto the roof of the temple as he sang. The hymn had seven verses, each sung in a different melody and repeated four times. At the conclusion of the hymn, the priest descended and re-entered the temple.

Next, the seven men who had driven the evil spirits from the town dipped seven white gourds into the medicine which had been brewing on the sacred fire. Then, each handed a gourd full of medicine to the head man of his own clan who drank from it and handed it on. As it passed from person to person, each drank and rubbed some on his chest. After all had partaken, the hymn to *Yowa* was repeated.

The usual ritual bathing and sacrifice followed. By this time it was sunset, and the *Yowa* hymn was sung again. A feast was then served, and during the evening the women joined in the Friendship Dance.

The rituals of the second and third days were the same, except that the *Yowa* hymn was not sung. The fourth day was a repetition of the first day, including the *Yowa* hymn. On the fifth and last day the medicine basket was withdrawn from the vessel and stored in a secret place. The ceremony was concluded when the officials and priests left, saying as they made their exit, "Now I depart." The people followed, holding in their hearts a deep sense of security and peace.

Bounding Bush Ceremony

Few details are known concerning the sixth annual ceremony.

It appears to have been a non-religious affair that featured dancing and feasting. In the main dance, men and women alternated in pairs. The two leaders, who were men, carried hoops having four spokes, to the ends of which white feathers were fastened. Other pairs in the center and at the end of the dancing column also carried hoops. All of the remaining couples carried white pine boughs in their right hands. The dance movement was circular, and in the center was a man with a small box. He danced around within the circle, singing as he did so, and as he passed by the dancers, each dropped a piece of tobacco into the box. This dance, which ended at midnight, was repeated on three successive nights.

On the fourth night, a feast preceded the dancing which did not begin until after midnight. This time, when the man with the box appeared, the people dropped pine needles in the box. At the conclusion of the dance near daylight, all of the dancers formed a circle around the altar fire. One by one, they advanced three times toward the fire, the third time tossing both tobacco and pine needles into the flames.

Symbolic sacrifice appears to have been the theme of this ceremony, but too few of its details have been preserved for its true meaning to be understood. It concluded the six great annual ceremonies, although at each new moon during the year there were minor local observances.

The Uku Dance

Every seventh year, the chief of the Cherokee nation led his people in a thanksgiving ceremony of great rejoicing. It was called the *Uku* dance because the chief, whose title was Uku, was at this time reconsecrated in his office of high priest. Uku was one of several titles conferred upon him. During the "Friends Made" ceremony, for example, his title meant "one who renews heart and body."

When the Uku dance occurred, it replaced the Great New Moon Ceremony. The customary seven days of preparation pre-

ceded it, and on the evening of the last day, the chief's seven
counselors took charge and appointed individuals to perform
special tasks. Among these were men to direct the feast and
women to cook the food. The "Honored Woman" was responsible
for warming water with which two of the counselors were to
bathe the chief. Another counselor was selected to disrobe him,
and still another to dress him in a ceremonial costume. Three additional appointments included a musician to lead the singing,
an attendant to fan the chief, and a third to build two elevated
seats, one in the square ground and the other between the temple
and the chief's home. These seats were tall, throne-like platforms,
whitened with clay and protected by canopies.

The ceremony proper began the next morning with the seven
counselors going to the home of the chief where they met the
"Honored Woman" waiting with the warm water. After undress-
ing and bathing the chief, they arrayed him in the new costume.
His usual garments on ceremonial occasions were white, including his moccasins and feather headdress. But for this event, his
entire costume was dyed bright yellow.

Then the chief, carried on the back of one of the counselors,
was brought to the throne that stood between his home and the
temple. In this procession, several of the counselors preceded
the chief, the musician walked at one side, the fanner at the other,
and the rest followed. All except the one who carried the chief
sang as they advanced. After a short rest, during which the
chief was seated on the throne, they resumed their march to
the square ground. Arriving there, he was placed upon the second
throne where he would remain until the next day. During this
long vigil, he and his officials kept perfect silence, while the rest
of the people spent the night dancing in the temple.

Early the next morning, after the men of the tribe had assembled, the attendants lifted the chief from the throne and carried
him to a previously marked circle in the center of the square. Not
until then had his feet been allowed to touch the ground.
Within the sacred circle he began the Uku dance. Moving slowly

with great dignity he inclined his head to each spectator, who bowed to him in return. Outside the circle the officials followed in single file, imitating his steps. When the dance was finished he was again placed upon the white throne where, surrounded by his attendants, he remained until sunset. Meanwhile, the rest of the people enjoyed a feast. Late in the afternoon, food was brought to the chief and his counselors, after which he was car-

DANCE

OF THE

UKU

ried back to his home and disrobed. With the exception of the ritual bathing, the same performance was repeated on the next three days.

After the Uku's dance on the fourth day, he was reinvested with his religious and civil powers by his right-hand man, and the ceremony was concluded.

Although the religious behavior of peoples of different cultures, such as the prehistoric Cherokee, often includes rituals and beliefs incomprehensible to the outsider, religion among all peoples is the outgrowth of human desire for an orderly and understandable universe. Of all cultural achievements, religion is the most highly symbolic and is as necessary to mankind as food, water and air.

Suggestions for Further Reading

The following twenty-four titles are recommended for those who wish to increase their knowledge of the first Americans. Some of the books are technical, others semi-technical, and a few are non-technical.

BUSHNELL, G. H. S.
    1957   *Peru*. Frederick A. Praeger. New York.
          Account of the great Peruvian civilization, including Inca and pre-Inca cultures. Written for the average interested reader. Semi-technical.

CALDWELL, JOSEPH R., AND CATHERINE McCANN
    1941   *Irene Mound Site, Chatham County, Georgia*. Athens.
          A readable although technical account of a site occupied by temple mound Indians and also by earlier Indians.

DEUEL, THORNE
    1952   Hopewellian Communities in Illinois. *Scientific Papers*, Vol. V, *Illinois State Museum*. Springfield.
          A recent description of a number of Hopewellian sites in Illinois, including a general description of the Hopewellian culture. Semi-technical.

FAIRBANKS, CHARLES H.
    1956   Archeology of the Funeral Mound, Ocmulgee National Monument, Georgia. *National Park Service, Archeological Research Series*, Number Three. Washington.
          Account of the excavation of a mound of the temple mound period at one of the great prehistoric southeastern ceremonial centers. Includes a general description of the temple mound culture in Georgia. Technical.

FUNDABURK, EMMA LILA AND MARY DOUGLAS FOREMAN, EDITORS
    1957   *Sun Circles and Human Hands, The Southeastern Indians—Art and Industry*. Luverne, Alabama.
          A profusely illustrated compilation dealing with the artistic

products and handicrafts of the Indians of the southeastern United States. Text consists mainly of quotations from authoritative publications. Semi-technical.

GILBERT, WILLIAM H., JR.
  1937 The Eastern Cherokees. *Anthropological Papers*, No. 23, *Bureau of American Ethnology*, Bulletin 133. Washington.
        An account of the Eastern Band of Cherokee in North Carolina, including a description of ancient Cherokee life based upon John Howard Payne manuscripts. Technical.

GRIFFIN, JAMES B., EDITOR
  1952 *Archeology of Eastern United States.* University of Chicago Press. Chicago.
        A collection of twenty-eight essays by specialists in the archaeology of various areas east of the Rocky Mountains. Extensive bibliography. Semi-technical.

LEWIS, THOMAS M. N. AND MADELINE KNEBERG
  1946 *Hiwassee Island: An Archaeological Account of Four Tennessee Indian Peoples.* The University of Tennessee Press. Knoxville.
        Account of the excavation of a large Tennessee archaeological site which was inhabited successively by burial mound builders, early and late temple mound builders, and the Cherokee. Technical.

LEWIS, THOMAS M. N. AND MADELINE KNEBERG, EDITORS
  1954 *Ten Years of the Tennessee Archaeologist, Selected Subjects.* J. B. Graham. Chattanooga.
        This collection of articles, written by or for amateur archaeologists appeared in the journal of the Tennessee Archaeological Society, between 1944 and 1954. Non-technical.

MARTIN, PAUL S., GEORGE I. QUIMBY, AND DONALD COLLIER
  1947 *Indians Before Columbus.* The University of Chicago Press. Chicago.
        A summary of the archaeological cultures in North America, north of Mexico. Provides a general picture of the entire area over a twenty-thousand-year period. Semi-technical.

MOONEY, JAMES
  1900 Myths of the Cherokee. *Bureau of American Ethnology, Nineteenth Annual Report.* Washington.

The most comprehensive account of the Cherokee that is available. Includes extensive historical material as well as myths and a vocabulary of Cherokee words. Semi-technical.

MORLEY, SYLVANUS G.

1956 *The Ancient Maya.* 3rd edition revised by George W. Brainerd. Stanford University Press. Stanford.

An extensive account of the Maya—civilization, and achievements in art, architecture and science. Semi-technical.

RITCHIE, WILLIAM A.

1957 Traces of Early Man in the Northeast. *New York State Museum and Science Service,* Bulletin Number 358. Albany.

A recent summary of information on the Ice Age hunters in the northeastern United States. Technical.

SEARS, WILLIAM H.

1956 Excavations at Kolomoki Final Report. *University of Georgia Series in Anthropology,* No. 5. Athens.

The final summarizing report on the excavation of a great southeastern ceremonial site in southern Georgia. Technical.

SELLARDS, ELIAS H.

1952 *Early Man in America, A Study in Prehistory.* University of Texas Press. Austin.

A general summary of the information on the Ice Age hunters. Special emphasis upon the sites in the southwestern United States. Technical.

STIRLING, MATTHEW W.

1955 *Indians of the Americas, A Color-Illustrated Record.* National Geographic Society. Washington.

A superbly illustrated series of articles on the various Indian cultures of North America, including Middle American cultures. Non-technical.

SWANTON, JOHN R.

1922 Early History of the Creek Indians. *Bureau of American Ethnology,* Bulletin 73. Washington.

Historical accounts of the various tribes included in the Creek confederacy. Technical.

1928 Social Organization and Social Usages of the Indians of the Creek Confederacy. *Bureau of American Ethnology, Forty-second Annual Report.* Washington.

Historical analysis of the culture of the Indians of the Creek confederacy. Particular emphasis upon the social, political and religious aspects. Technical.

1946   The Indians of the Southeastern United States. *Bureau of American Ethnology*, Bulletin 137. Washington.

A source book of the historical cultures of the southeastern Indians, with a comprehensive bibliography. Semi-technical.

VAILLANT, GEORGE C.

1948   *Aztecs of Mexico, Origin, Rise and Fall of the Aztec Nation.* Doubleday & Co. Garden City.

Account of the Aztec and pre-Aztec cultures of Mexico. Semi-technical.

WEBB, WILLIAM S.

1938   An Archeological Survey of the Norris Basin in Eastern Tennessee. *Bureau of American Ethnology*, Bulletin 118. Washington.

Account of excavations of twenty-three sites in the Norris Basin, including caves, burial mounds and temple mounds. Technical.

1939   An Archeological Survey of Wheeler Basin on the Tennessee River in Northern Alabama. *Bureau of American Ethnology*, Bulletin 122. Washington.

Account of Wheeler Basin excavations, including Archaic, burial mound, and Mississippian period sites. Technical.

WEBB, WILLIAM S., AND DAVID DEJARNETTE

1942   An Archeological Survey of Pickwick Basin in Adjacent Portions of the States of Alabama, Mississippi, and Tennessee. *Bureau of American Ethnology*, Bulletin 129. Washington.

Account of excavations of Archaic burial mound and temple mound sites, mainly in Alabama. Over three hundred photographic plates. Technical.

WORMINGTON, H. MARIE

1957   Ancient Man in North America. *The Denver Museum of Natural History, Popular Series*, No. 4, fourth edition. Denver.

The most comprehensive account of Ice Age hunters in North America, with an extensive bibliography. Semi-technical.

Index